DATE DUE

GAYLORD			PRINTED IN U.S.A.

FEB 0 2 2007

THE COLLECTED POEMS OF EVELYN SCOTT

THE COLLECTED POEMS
OF EVELYN SCOTT

Edited, with Notes and an Introduction
by Caroline C. Maun

THE NATIONAL POETRY FOUNDATION

ORONO, MAINE 2005

09 08 07 06 05   1 2 3 4 5

Design: Betsy Rose and Michael Alpert. Cover: Martin Johnson Heade, *Giant Magnolias on a Blue Velvet Cloth*, c. 1890. Gift of the Circle of the National Gallery of Art in Commemoration of its 10th Anniversary. Photograph © Board of Trustees, National Gallery of Art, Washington, D.C. Used with permission.

The paper used in the publication meets the minimum requirements of the American National Standard for Information Sciences—Permanence of Paper for Printed Library Materials, ansi z39.48-1984.

The publication of this book was made possible in part by a grant from the Stephen and Tabitha King Foundation.

Library of Congress Cataloging-in-Publication Data

Scott, Evelyn, 1893–1963
    [Poems]
    The collected poems of Evelyn Scott / edited, with notes and an introduction by Caroline C. Maun. Preface by Burton Hatlen.
        p. cm.
    Includes bibliographical references and index.
    ISBN 0-943373-67-0 (alk. paper)
        I. Maun, Caroline C., 1968- II. Title.

PS3537.C89 A6 2002
811'.52--dc21   2002035694

For Robert Welker,
in tribute to his generous and pioneering spirit

CONTENTS

*

Precipitations

The Winter Alone

The Gravestones Wept

PART I   143

Previously Uncollected Poems

*

ACKNOWLEDGMENTS

For permission to print from manuscript materials I gratefully acknowledge Evelyn Scott's literary executrix Paula Scott, The University of Tennessee at Knoxville Special Collections Library, and the Harry Ransom Humanities Research Center of the University of Texas at Austin. As a graduate student doing doctoral research that contributed to this volume, I benefited from the release time made possible by the John B. Emperor Fellowship at The University of Tennessee, and my travel to the University of Texas was supported by a Durant da Ponte American Literature Fellowship in 1997 from The University of Tennessee Department of English. Librarians at both institutions were very helpful in this project, especially Rachel Howarth of the Harry Ransom Humanities Research Center, and Bill Eigelsbach of The University of Tennessee Special Collections Library.

Dorothy M. Scura, as my dissertation director at University of Tennessee, has been involved in this project since its inception and has provided unflagging support and crucial guidance. She has shown me through example what scholarship should be. Robert Welker, who preserved many of the Evelyn Scott papers, has been of tremendous influence in my work and in the work of others who are endeavoring to recover Scott for a wider readership. I spent many exhilarating days reading Scott's papers at his home in Huntsville, Alabama before he donated them to The University of Tennessee Special Collections Library; I am indebted to his generosity, hospitality, and friendship. From 1998 until 2004, at Morgan State University, I enjoyed the support and friendship of the Chairperson of English and Language Arts, Dolan Hubbard. Since 2004 I thank the Chairperson of the Interdisciplinary Studies Department at Wayne State University, Stuart Henry, for his support. I also thank at Wayne State University Robin Boyle, Julie Klein, Lisa Maruca, Jim Michaels, Dick Raspa, and Roz Schindler. For the gifts of their friendship and encouragement in this project I thank: Jewell Chambers, Dahli Gray, John Kress, B. J. Leggett, James Lloyd, Mary Jane Lupton, Karen Overbye, Art Smith, Joseph Trahern, Mary Wheeling White, and Minnie Washington.

For standing by and believing, I thank most of all my mother, Laurette M. Maun.

During the past decade, the National Poetry Foundation has taken as one of its tasks the recovery of certain "lost" poets of the twentieth century: poets who enjoyed significant literary reputations during their lifetimes but who have, for one reason or another, disappeared from sight. Thus we have published volumes by Kenneth Fearing, Parker Tyler, and Stuart Z. Perkoff, with the goal of giving these poets a "second chance." Our edition of the *Collected Poems of Evelyn Scott* continues this series of volumes by "recovered" poets. We anticipate that this volume will be followed by editions of the poetry of Helen Adam and Lola Ridge.

Born in 1893 and beginning her writing career in the late 1910s, Evelyn Scott belongs to a generation that radically and permanently transformed the role of women poets within American culture. Other members of this generation include Gertrude Stein, Lola Ridge and Amy Lowell, all about twenty years older than Scott; Sara Teasdale, Elinor Wylie, H.D., Marianne Moore, and Mina Loy, all about a decade older than Scott; Edna St. Vincent Millay, Babette Deutsch, and Genevieve Taggard, almost exact contemporaries of Scott; and Laura Riding, Leonie Adams, Louise Bogan, Marya Zaturenska, Kay Boyle, and Lorine Niedecker, all from five to ten years younger than Scott. Among these poets, Stein, H.D., and Moore today have achieved unquestioned canonical status, while Loy, Riding, and Niedecker have devoted followings among experimental poets. Millay, who enjoyed a large popular audience during her lifetime but then slipped out of the anthologies, is today making a comeback. As one criterion of current literary status, it is worth noting that Stein, Lowell, H.D., Moore, Millay, Taggard, and Bogan (the last two perhaps mildly surprising choices) are all included in the sixth edition of *The Norton Anthology of American Literature*. In another current anthology, *Twentieth-Century American Poetry*, edited by Dana Gioia and others, Taggard disappears, while Teasdale and Wylie are added. Otherwise the women poets listed above do not find a place within the current American canon. And several poets in my list of the "generation of 1900" (Ridge, Deutsch, Zaturenska, Adams) have "disappeared" almost as completely as has Scott. With Elizabeth Bishop, born in 1911, and Muriel Rukeyser, born in 1913, we come to a new generation.

Within the company of women poets among whom I have situated her, Scott is perhaps the most extreme "case"; for after enjoying a brief period of fame and even authoring a bestseller, in her later years she found it impossible to publish her work, and she was labeled as "mad" by several of her contemporaries. However, the stresses that she experienced were in fact common to this entire group of writers, and in this respect her story helps us to understand the career paths of the others as well.

Sexual rebellion is a common pattern along all the members of this generation of women poets. Stein, H.D., Millay, and probably others were lesbian or bisexual. In *Being Geniuses Together*, Kay Boyle memorably recounts the story of her erotic adventures, including a period of unbridled promiscuity. And in the context of the 1920s, isn't even Moore's adamant celibacy a form of rebellion? In company with many of her contemporaries, Scott felt a new freedom to explore her own sexuality. In her introduction to this volume, Caroline Maun records some of Scott's erotic adventures, and to these I would add Scott's brief but intense love affair with William Carlos Williams. In her poetry Scott rarely refers to specific erotic experiences, but she does set out to explore a full range of sensory possibilities, and in this respect her poetry participates in a liberatory project that permanently (unless the mullahs of the Islamic and Christian worlds succeed in undoing the women's revolution) changed Western civilization. Yet the attempt to define new modes of self-definition for women was not without its costs for the members of this generation: examples include Teasdale's suicide and Millay's alcoholism, along with Scott's "madness." (However, I'm not sure that the record for male poets of this generation is much more auspicious: witness the alcoholism of Winters and many others, Crane's suicide, etc.)

The women poets in the "generation of 1900" also broke new ground by pursuing independent professional careers *as writers*. The one indisputably great woman poet of the nineteenth century, Emily Dickinson, was supported throughout her life by her affluent father, and thus never needed to worry about earning a livelihood. Of course, some nineteenth-century women managed to make a living as writers, but the list isn't long. And a later generation of women writers, beginning with Bishop, Rukeyser, and their contemporaries, often found modest financial security within universities. But as far as I know, only Boyle, who outlived all the other writers I've listed, eventually found a home in a university. For most of the writers of the "generation of 1900," how to make a living was a paramount problem. Niedecker, for instance, worked for a time as a cleaning woman in a hospital. Like others among her contemporaries, Scott was a free-lance professional writer, with no source of a livelihood except her pen. She wrote novels because they brought in income, while she wrote poetry for herself. However, in all of her work she was trying to be faithful to her own artistic sense, even as she sought a mass audience. But then in the 1930s and 1940s, as the middlebrow audience that had made Scott's 1929 novel *The Wave* a bestseller disappeared, she found herself destitute. In the meantime, Deutsch and Bogan, for example, found niches within the world of magazine publishing, but Scott's increasingly evident eccentricity closed off such options.

From this perspective, Bogan's condescending portrait of Scott, as quoted in Caroline Maun's introduction to this volume, takes on a certain irony: as poetry editor of *The New Yorker*, Bogan enjoyed a steady income, whereas Scott was truly destitute—and frantic. The letters from "Cress" (in real life, Marcia Nardi) that Williams incorporates into *Paterson* offer a parallel case. Like Scott, Cress is trying to survive as a self-employed woman writer during the 1940s, and as we read her letters it becomes clear that many of the people whom she meets see her as "mad"—although to his credit Williams does not. And if the personal traumas of these years turned both Scott and Cress into "cases," we might well ask what would have become of H.D., if Bryher had not provided an environment in which she could thrive as a writer.

Along with the perils of both personal and economic independence, many of the women writers of the Generation of 1900 were traumatized by the mounting violence of the twentieth century. In this respect Virginia Woolf's suicide at the beginning of World War II is paradigmatic: she simply could not endure the prospect of living through all that violence again. H.D.'s breakdown of 1945 was also directly related to the trauma of the war, but in *Trilogy* and *Helen in Egypt* she found ways of transforming the horror into great art. Kay Boyle, but in her fiction rather than her poetry, also created imaginative structures that were in some measure adequate to the experience of the war. Others, including especially Millay, tried to create such structures, but failed. As for Scott, her foreword to the 1951 version of *The Gravestones Wept* (see Appendix B to this volume) suggests how profoundly shaken she was by the war, so that in some ways Scott seems as much a casualty of World War II as the soldiers who died at Omaha Beach. Did she find a way of transforming the experience of the war into art? Certainly not on the scale of H.D., but some of her poems from the period of the war (see especially 191–201 in this volume) offer vivid and poignant images of the war years.

The pathos of Scott's life—a pathos on which she insisted more and more stridently as she became older—is clear enough. But what of the poetry itself? Is there any reason to resurrect it? To answer this question, we need to explore briefly the aesthetic choices she faced, as a young poet in the second decade of the twentieth century. In the years immediately after World War I, when Scott began writing poetry, three admired poets among Scott's immediate predecessors and contemporaries, Teasdale, Wylie, and Millay, offered one powerful model for the aspiring woman poet. In labeling this tradition "sentimental," I do not mean to derogate the work of these poets. Teasdale and Wylie both had fine ears for the music of the English language and an extraordinary dexterity in the use of traditional forms. Furthermore, as Suzanne Clark points out in her brilliant *Sentimental Modernism: Women Writers and the Revolution of the Word* (Indiana University Press, 1991), poets like Teasdale, Wylie, and Millay preserved a place within poetry for love (as distinct from sex) and for personal feeling generally, at a time when these possibilities were under attack from a Modernist aesthetic that idealized the objective and the impersonal. In this respect, as Clark argues, the work of these poets represented a form of feminist resistance to an increasingly oppressive masculinist aesthetic.

Scott clearly identified in some measure with what was increasingly becoming a women's sentimental tradition, as she sought to preserve a place for the personal in her poetry. In this respect, however, it is important to recognize the significance of Scott's enduring loyalty to Lola Ridge, to whom she addressed at least three poems (see 47, 117, and 168). (Ridge reciprocated by writing at least one poem to Scott, in *Red Flag*.) For Ridge's poetry offers an alternative to the obsessive circling about the authorial ego that ultimately vitiates the work of the sentimental poets. (Teasdale, in many ways the most elegant of the group, is also the most debilitatingly self-centered.) Rather Ridge pioneered a mode of women's poetry that turned outward toward the world, and Scott followed her mentor in this respect. Just as Ridge offered a richly detailed portrait of life in the New York ghetto, so Scott, within her poetry at least, is less interested in her own sufferings than in the people she meets and the places she visits.

Along with the poetry of Ridge, a major influence on Scott's work was her experiences within what we might call, uniting two terms that Ezra Pound introduced into literary discourse, the Imagist Vortex. When Scott began to write poetry, she published in journals (*Others, Poetry*) identified with Imagism, and Scott's early poetry suggests that she committed herself to an Imagist aesthetic far more strongly than any of the immediate age-mates (i.e., Millay, Taggard, and Deutsch) among whom I have situated her. Thus her early poetry remains of interest for what it reveals about the resources of such an aesthetic. In the years just after World War I, H.D. and Amy Lowell offered contrasting models of how a woman poet might adapt an Imagist aesthetic for her own ends, and as a model Scott opted for the relatively rigorous H.D. over the loquacious Lowell. But William Carlos Williams was perhaps an even more compelling model. Here are the opening lines of "Destiny," a poem by Scott first published in 1918: "I am lost in the vast cave of night. / No sound but the far-off tinkle of stars, / And the cry of a bird / Muffled in shadows." The claim to situate us in the here and now and to evoke the immediacy of experience through a mildly startling metaphor dislocation (stars don't, of course, "tinkle")—these rhetorical strategies are the stock in trade of Williams' early poetry, as collected in *Al Que Quiere!* (1917) and *Sour Grapes* (1921).

A reading of Scott's 1920 volume *Precipitations* in the context of H.D.'s *Sea Garden* and Williams' poems before *Spring and All* (his more radically experimental 1923 volume) suggests the degree to which all three poets shared a common period style. Scott's metaphoric twists are perhaps a shade more ornate than H.D.'s, and we do not find in her work the syntactic ruptures through which Williams increasingly sought to shock us into new modes of perception. But like the poets (including H.D. and Williams) of Pound's *Des Imagistes* anthology, Scott aspired to what Emerson called an "original relationship with the universe," and her language retains a freshness and immediacy that I do not find in the work of such lesser participants in the Imagist Vortex as, say, James Gould Fletcher or Maxwell Bodenheim—or, for that matter, Amy Lowell.

But in *Precipitations* we find qualities of vision that are distinctly Scott's own, and that make the book something more than an example of a period style. The sequence of hospital poems grouped under the title "The Red Cross" (18–20 in this volume) explores the experience of delirium in a way that seems to me unique. Scott also displays from early on a novelist's ability to give herself over fully to the observation of people and places. The true "otherness" of the Brazilian landscape comes through strongly in the poems set in that country (50–57). Consider this understated but chilling image of a snake: "The chickens are at home in the barnyard, / The pigs in the swill, / And the flowers in the garden; / But where do you belong, / With your lacquered coils, / O Snake?" And Scott, to a degree rare among the poets of her generation, regularly speaks from and to the life experiences specifically of women—see, for example, most of the poems on pages 41 to 47 in this volume. "The Maternal Breast" (16) anticipates a theme we've come to associate with Adrienne Rich: "I walked straight and long, / But I never found you. / I was looking for a hill of a hundred breasts, / A hill modeled after the statues of Diana of the Ephesians. / I was looking for a hill of mounds hairy with grass, / And a place to lie down." The experiences of women include motherhood, and the sequence titled "The Tunnel" (24–26) courageously confronts the ambivalences of the mother/child relationship.

Precipitations remains, then, a small but eloquent testament to the poetic energies released within the Imagist Vortex. But like all poets of her generation (the one exception may be Charles Reznikoff, who remained throughout his life faithful to the Imagist aesthetic), Scott had to find a way forward from Imagism. Her second collection of poems, *The Winter Alone* (1930), suggests the difficulties of this project. We find here few of the short poems characteristic of the first book, each of them seeking to capture a flash of immediate perception, but no clear alternative aesthetic has emerged. The Imagism of the first book has not, in fact, disappeared; rather it has become looser and more diffuse. But *The Winter Alone* does offer at least one section that carries us toward something new: in a section titled "Impervious Friends" (89–102 in this volume), Scott has created a series of witty and incisive animal portraits. These poems may be influenced by a third member of the Modernist group of poets who were about ten years older than Scott, Marianne Moore. By 1924 Moore had published "Peter" (a portrait of a friend's cat) and "Dock Rats"; and Scott's animal poems rival Moore's in their scrupulous attention to detail and their eagerness to give themselves over wholly to the things and creatures of this world, thereby transcending the subjectivizing I/eye. Some of the human portraits in *The Winter Alone* are no less delightful—see, for example, "Chopin's Grave Revisited" (103 in this volume). *The Winter Alone* also offers many memorable images of women at various stages in their life journeys. The "Chopin's Grave" poem, for example, offers a vignette of girlhood, while "Aphrodite in Winter" (111) confronts the painful realities of aging. We also find Scott experimenting with some new possibilities in this volume, as in "A Newspaper Ballad" (113–15), an exploration of a satirical voice that will become increasingly important later in her career.

The troubled poetic career of H.D.—who had apparently come to a dead end with *Red Roses for Bronze* (1931), publishing virtually no poetry for a decade thereafter— suggests the difficulties of creating a poetics that would be faithful to the experimental impulse of Imagism, while moving beyond the limitations of an Imagist poetics. H.D., of course, found her way to the great long poems of the World War II years and after. We see no comparable achievement in Scott's career, but her third collection of poems, *The Gravestones Wept*, represents a courageous attempt to forge a post-Imagist poetics that will do justice to the complexities of historical experience, in the darkening years of the 1930s and after. *The Gravestones Wept* has remained heretofore unpublished, and in bringing this volume into print our primary goal is to allow readers to judge for themselves these late poems by Scott and to see the poems in the context of Scott's poetic development from 1918, when she first began publishing poetry, to the end of her life.

While by the 1940s some of Scott's erstwhile friends judged her as "mad," the poems that she wrote during the 1930s and 1940s seem eminently lucid and controlled. The long opening sequence of *The Gravestones Wept*, "Woman Cycle" (143–52), introduces a new, personal note into Scott's verse. Yet while it is clearly autobiographical, the sequence is not "confessional" in the mode that became fashionable among American poets of the 1950s, for the persona speaks as "Everywoman," rather than specifically as Evelyn Scott. In this respect Scott's poetry is closer to that of Adrienne Rich than it is to the poetry of, say, Anne Sexton. Several of these late poems have a vigorous satirical edge, as Scott addresses herself to the corruptions of American consumer culture: see, for example, "Old American Stock," about the 1939 New York World's Fair (154 ff.), "On Behalf of the Inarticulate" (163 ff.), and "Wax Works" (183–84). Rhyme serves Scott well in these satiric poems, allowing her to twist her language toward epigrammatic closure: "The sun ascending to full noon / Burns mystery from Pharaoh's tomb / And shines delightfully on Franklin D., / Whose public smile for you and me / Presages reportorial hours / When Mrs. Roosevelt at his heel / Will brood successes like some ardent female seal" (183).

In her various prefaces to *The Gravestones Wept*, Scott worried obsessively about the presence or absence of a specifically Christian dimension in these late poems; but rather than imposing on us dogmatic demands, the poems use Christian symbolism—as, indeed, Scott had done throughout her career, as in the "Coming of Christ" sequence in *Precipitations* (59 ff.)—to add resonance to the mundane details of everyday life. More pertinent to understanding what makes these late poems unique is a poem titled "To the Mocked Romantics" and dated 1955. This poem suggests that in her later years Scott increasingly sought a poetic model in the work of the Romantics, so often scorned by the Modernists who had dominated the poetic world of the 1920s. And indeed, in many of these late poems Scott seems to be trying to recover something of the breadth of vision and the linguistic resonance characteristic of the Romantics—qualities that the minimalist aesthetic of Imagism had deliberately sought to exclude from poetry.

This return to the Romantics means at times a return to characteristic Romantic forms. Scott's satiric poems are, perhaps, Byronic in inspiration, and the memorable "Pike's Peak" (159-60) represents a noble effort at the Romantic ode, on the model perhaps of Shelley's "Mont Blanc." In the 1930s and 1940s Scott also composed a considerable number of sonnets, and these too look back to Romantic antecedents, perhaps via the sonnets of Edwin Arlington Robinson and Robert Frost. A return to traditional forms was, of course, widespread in the 1930s and 1940s: see, for example, the career paths of Yvor Winters and Allen Tate. But it seems important to emphasize that Scott's move from free verse to "closed" forms is not simply a response to fashion. She wants, like H.D. in these same years, to recover ancient values that the war and the general frenzy of modernity threatened to destroy, but without retreating to the dead-end, ego-centered sentimentality of Teasdale, Wylie, or Millay. For Scott as for these other women poets, traditional forms affirm a possibility of an organic order that will preserve a place for human feeling. But for Teasdale or Millay such forms too easily became an habitual gesture, whereas Scott's sonnets are never merely a mechanical working through of a system of arbitrary rules— rather each poem seems rescued from chaos by a sheer act of the will. In this respect these poems sometimes remind me of the handful of poems that Yvor Winters offered as his bulwark against the tides of undisciplined feeling. But unlike Winters, Scott does not repudiate the aspirations of her earlier poetry. Rather she wants to carry forward in a new way the immediacy of vision apparent in *Precipitations*, and in this respect Scott's late work represents, at moments in any case, a triumphant fusion of Modernity and Tradition.

Here, as a final example, is a sonnet from 1942, titled "Toward Home," about the difficulty and the possibility of recovering the vision we need to sustain us:

> As slowly, upon every lifting height,
> Stand forth odd symmetries of rock and shale,
> Down gilded valleys flows the fragrant gale,
> And the ascending, many-petaled light
> Again accords the mind the gift of sight;
> While ponderings, by multitudes made stale
> Elude the blight of the repeated tale
> And wrest from commonplace the unique right
> To lands Villon, Verlaine and Heine knew.
> Midst basking fields, all silver-sleek with dew,
> Keats's batter'd casement is flung wide
> On recent battle-ground and blood-soaked tide.
> Alas, for ancient, chartless fairy foam—
> How like a stranger's is our road toward home!

With this book, so ably assembled by Caroline Maun, Scott has, at last, I would like to believe, found her road home.

–Burton Hatlen
Director, National Poetry Foundation

INTRODUCTION

Elsie Dunn, later known as Evelyn Scott, was born in January 1893 to Maude Thomas and Seely Dunn of Clarksville, Tennessee. Her father worked for the Louisville and Nashville Railroad as a railroad superintendent, moved on to work as a train dispatcher, and later became involved in building railroads. Her mother's family had been established in Clarksville since 1829, when Elsie's great-grandfather, Captain Joseph Thomas, settled in the vicinity. His son, Maude's father Edwin Thomas, freed his slaves and was a non-combatant in the Civil War. By the time of Elsie's birth, the situation of the Dunn Family was typical of much of the southern gentry—rich in land and house, but poor in money. For a time the Dunn family lived in Russelville, Kentucky, then St. Louis, Missouri. Finally they settled, when Elsie Dunn was 14, in New Orleans to be near her paternal grandparents.

From an early age, Elsie displayed an interest in artistic creation and writing. As a young girl she kept an elaborate scrapbook that recorded the theater life of New Orleans. While still a teenager, she displayed her progressive bent of mind by working as secretary for the Women's Suffrage Party of Louisiana. She attended the Sophie Newcombe Preparatory School, the Sophie Newcombe Art School, and then Tulane University for a brief period. This period is given special attention by the author in her autobiography *Background in Tennessee* (1937). She credits her Southern upbringing with providing her much of her artistic material and fostering her sensibility as a writer.

On the day after Christmas 1913, just under a month before her twenty-first birthday, Elsie Dunn left New Orleans with Frederick Creighton Wellman, then Dean of the School of Tropical Medicine at Tulane University. Wellman had met Elsie's father in Honduras when Seely Dunn was working on railroad projects. From New Orleans Elsie and Wellman took a train to Biloxi, Mississippi, and then went on to New York, London, and Rio de Janeiro. On the way out of the States the couple shed their identities and became Cyril Kay-Scott and Evelyn Scott. Because Cyril's wife would not grant him a divorce, their relationship remained a common-law marriage. Although she was never completely out of touch with her family,

Scott's act was considered extreme and profoundly affected her subsequent life.

Scott's autobiographical novel *Escapade* (1923) describes the first three years of her six years in Brazil with Cyril. *Escapade* describes the extreme poverty, isolation, and hardship of the narrator, Evelina (Scott herself), and her relationships to her "husband," John (Cyril); her son, Jackie (Creighton, born in Recife on October 26, 1914); and her "aunt," Nannette (Scott's mother, Maude Thomas Dunn, who joined Evelyn and Cyril in Brazil). The true identities of the characters are veiled because of the potentially volatile nature of the narrative. Evelyn's father, Seely Dunn, divorced her mother, Maude Thomas Dunn, for desertion after he purposefully failed to provide her a means to get back to New Orleans from Brazil. As a result of these events, Evelyn suffered a breach with her family that was never fully repaired. Although she was close to her mother until Maude's death in April 1940, she became estranged from her grandparents and her father, a situation that caused her pain, but never remorse, for the actions she had taken. Besides living the experiences that informed *Escapade*, while in Brazil Scott began to compose her play *Love* (produced in New York in 1921), and to send poems to American and British "Little Magazines," such as Harriet Monroe's *Poetry*.

In her lifetime, Scott was best known as a novelist rather than as a poet. Along with the autobiographical *Escapade* of 1923, Scott published a trilogy of naturalistic novels in the early 1920s: *The Narrow House* (1921), *Narcissus* (1922) and *The Golden Door* (1925). The 1921–25 trilogy explored dysfunctional power structures in the family and was informed by psychological probing and stream of consciousness writing. Scott followed this first trilogy with a trilogy of panoramic historical novels: *Migrations* (1927), *The Wave* (1929) and *Calendar of Sin* (1931). While the first trilogy focuses on the individual and the self, in the historical trilogy Scott expands her canvas to portray a century of change and development from the antebellum period in the South to 1914. Some of the characters in these novels are based on members of Scott's family, and many important scenes take place in Tennessee. *The Wave*, a best-seller, became Scott's most critically acclaimed work, and it remains important in literary history in part because of its tremendously ambitious structure. Composed of many short-story length vignettes, the novel focuses on the Civil War as an event that affects nearly a hundred lives. Non-partisan with regard to the North or the South, the novel reflected Scott's own mixed cultural heritage.

The years from 1930 onward saw a slow decline both in the critical acclaim that Scott's novels received and in their sales. Although her novels continued to be reviewed well, Scott would never again achieve the recognition that she received with *The Wave* in 1929, and as the years wore on she had fewer and fewer financial and emotional resources with which to promote her work. In her novels *Breathe Upon These Slain* (1934), *Bread and a Sword* (1937), and *Shadow of the Hawk* (1941), Scott turned to a three-part examination of the plight of the artist in society, a theme in which she felt a keen personal interest. In her personal life, Evelyn Scott and Cyril Kay-Scott dissolved their common-law marriage by divorce in 1928, and Scott married British novelist John Metcalfe in 1930.

In 1941 Scott's final published novel, *The Shadow of the Hawk*, appeared. It had a very limited circulation. Scott composed two more novels, *Escape into Living* and *Before Cock Crow*, which remain unpublished. Scott's later years were characterized by a chronic need for money, breaches of contact with many of her family members, and an increasing paranoia about political events during the Second World War and the effects of these events on artists.

Although throughout her career as a writer Scott concentrated her primary energies on fiction writing, her identity as a poet was important to her from her literary debut in 1918 until the end of her career. Scott initiated her career as a poet by publishing "Moon Cycle" from Brazil in *Poetry Journal*. In 1919 and 1920, Scott published poetry in the most important literary magazines of the period, including *Others*, *Poetry*, and *The Dial*. These poems defined her as an Imagist and a Modernist whose primary subjects were subjectivity, sexuality, and the exotic Brazilian locales that catalyzed her writing from 1913 until 1919. In 1920 she published a collection of poems, *Precipitations*, which included these early magazine-published poems, along with many additional poems exploring urban life, race relations, sexual politics, and nature.

In a 1958 dissertation, Robert Welker describes *Precipitations* as "filled with verbal shocks, sudden shifts in meaning, and surprising images, sometimes confused, sometimes strained. . . . There is a complete avoidance of abstract statement and an extreme honesty of emotional expression."[1] He cites examples of what he sees as "pure Imagism" ("The Storm," "From Brooklyn," and "Ship Masts"), and he emphasizes poems showing "an honest insight into terror and spiritual grandeur" (Welker 151). According to Welker, the poems in *Precipitations* develop an overarching theme of *liebestod*, as they "offer the record of an insight into experience which unifies life and death. . . . The victory over life and experience which these poems represent . . . may be called 'Gothic,' a term first applied to Evelyn Scott by Waldo Frank. . . . It represents a victory over life which, forever aware of human destiny in death, sees death as the ultimate goal. It sees the grinning head of a skull as a smile of joy and peace" (Welker 153). In her recent biography of Scott, Mary Wheeling White focuses on Scott's cycle poems published in periodicals prior to the publication of *Precipitations*.[2] She emphasizes the erotic imagery and themes of female subjectivity in these poems, and she identifies H.D. as a strong influence on Scott. She also emphasizes the distinctive qualities of Scott's imagery in these early poems: "[In 1920, Scott's] set of thirteen poems entitled 'Tropical Life' appeared in *Poetry*, the premier stage for new American and European verse. This cycle overflows with unencumbered, often witty impressions of the earthy life Scott had led in Brazil. Images of overripe decay in the midst of lush vegetative fecundity figure prominently and would continue to show up in her later literature" (White 43). Early reviewers were in accord with both Welker's and White's observations of the poems in *Precipitations*. Scott is identified as a Modernist by Padraic Colum, Mark Van Doren, and Lola Ridge, in reviews of the book which appeared in *The New Republic*, *The Nation*, and *Poetry*.[3] They pointed out the isolated personae of the poems, Scott's use of open forms, and her exploration of unconventional subject matter.

Scott's second volume of poetry, *The Winter Alone*, published in 1930, shows the influence of her travels to Bermuda and Beziers, North Africa, in much the same way as *Precipitations* is evocative of Scott's Brazilian experience. The primary thematic development in *The Winter Alone* is a sustained investigation of a disillusionment that accompanies the renewal of life in spring. Through this focus, Scott was able to continue to explore the interrelationship of life and death begun in *Precipitations*. The first section, "Bright World," includes poems describing the renewal of the world through generation, but the force of generation seems sluggish, only reluctantly shaking off stagnancy and inertia. The speaker in the poems is an astute observer of her natural surroundings, and she is able to pick up intimations—although nothing more substantial than that—of the larger forces which animate nature. The speaker responds to new life, to the moon, to the ocean, and to her own body through the use of unexpected identifications.

In *The Winter Alone* there is a marked increase in instances of direct address to the reader, in calls to action or to notice some thing, and in the use of exclamation marks, trends which continue in her later poetry. Scott uses these devices to create a more urgent, even a strident, tone. This tendency will eventually evolve into full-blown protest poetry in *The Gravestones Wept*. In its formal aspects, the poetry in *The Winter Alone* may be characterized as mostly open; the use of rhyme is sparing, and when used it is deployed freely so as not to become a predictable feature. The poems are constructed to highlight through rhythm the juxtaposition of unlike concepts and surprising comparisons.

The *Winter Alone* was not widely reviewed. With the coming of the Great Depression, the subjectivity that Scott was exploring was becoming unfashionable, and critics seemed uncertain how to deal with a volume of poems by the author of a best-selling novel. However, in *The Nation* Eda Lou Walton praised the subject matter of the poems, the "intricate emotional situations" and "vivid backgrounds" (350). Among later critics, Mary Wheeling White connects *The Winter Alone* to the themes of female subjectivity and gender developed in her discussion of *Precipitations*. White also reports that Scott was pleased with *The Winter Alone*, telling Lola Ridge that it was "a kind of portrait of the author—like *Escapade* in poetry with factual sequences omitted" (132).

Evelyn Scott's third and last book of poetry, *The Gravestones Wept*, is a collection of fifty-one poems begun in 1931 and completed in 1960. During those years Scott reshaped and edited the volume at least four separate times. Although it has never been published, it received the benefit of Scott's attention and thought over a longer period than many of her published works. In it Scott continues her Modernist investigations of the themes and subjects which she had explored in her two earlier books of poetry. *The Gravestones Wept*, however, is more comprehensive and detailed in scope than her earlier books of poetry, perhaps because it evolved over a lengthier period of time, so that the book reflects Scott's central concerns during the last three decades of her life.

During the years that Scott composed *The Gravestones Wept*, she experienced perpetual economic hardship. During the late forties and fifties Scott felt that she must take advantage of any platform to tell her unfortunate story, and *The Gravestones Wept* presented no exception. The crux of her crisis was this: Scott found herself estranged first from her father, then from her ex-husband, whom she still respected and admired after their divorce, and finally from her son and his family. Scott wrote hundreds of letters to friends and colleagues telling her story, wrote an autobiographical "Précis" which was intended for use to supplement legal testimony should a trial regarding the settlement of her father's estate ever arise, and published a lengthy "Preface" dealing with cultural and political issues and the artist in her novel *Bread and a Sword*.[4]

The last thirty years of Scott's life were indeed years of strife. Key events which play a part in the subject matter of the poems, and which are reflected in the supplemental material she included with various versions of it, include Scott's brief war-time conversion to Catholicism and subsequent separation from the Church; peregrinations from the United States to Canada to Britain to join her husband, John Metcalfe, a Royal Air Force officer; disagreements and misunderstandings with her son, Creighton Scott, and his family, which would persist until the end of her life; and extreme, unrelenting poverty. During a four-year period in which she lived separately from her husband, Scott sought solace in religious conversion. She had been born in Tennessee into the Episcopal faith, but her particular development tended more toward rationalism and philosophy than faith and religion. Her mid-life sojourn with God she later deemed a product of impulse and an effect of the war. She broke with the church after less than a year as a member, and she is at pains in her "Foreword" to *The Gravestones Wept* to make the circumstances absolutely clear.[5] In her desire to believe and then her resistance to faith, we can see Scott striving for order and coherence in the face of chaos, but also rejecting answers that came to her, she felt, too easily. Scott began to link her unpleasant rift with the church to her inability to publish as she would like to. In fact, earlier versions of poems in *The Gravestones Wept* show evidence of being more concerned with religious issues than are the later, edited versions. But if the war drove her to the church, certainly it drove her artistic efforts as well. A key influence on poems in *The Gravestones Wept* is the fighting of World War II. In June of 1944 Scott joined Metcalfe in London, where she experienced the last of the V-1 bombings and the full round of V-2 bombings, and her poems are colored by those experiences of war.

In addition to these vicissitudes, Scott's peace of mind through this time was complicated by a paranoia that worked against her as she tried to maneuver in the publishing world. Scott's correspondence, business and personal, is voluminous, and she became bewildered and angry as her list of unanswered letters grew ever longer. Stoking the paranoia was the fact that many of her correspondents were breaking contact with her because of emotional and monetary demands she made on them, but Scott was fueled by these circumstances to suspect foul play and third-party interference with the mail. There were many unfortunate consequences of Scott's increasing paranoia; for example, she so exasperated her literary agent for *The Gravestones Wept*, Virginia Rice, with tales of her difficulties with the mail that Rice backed off the project in November of 1949.[6] From that point on Scott had to represent *The Gravestones Wept* by herself, with the sometime help of several literary friends in New York. Serving as her own agent was additionally difficult for her because she had no money even for postage. For a time in London, Scott dropped out of circulation completely for want of anything to wear in public (White 210).

Two remarkable portraits of Scott have been provided by other women poets, one from midway through her career and one from late in her career. Both portraits shed light on Scott as a person and an artist. In a memoir co-authored with Robert McAlmon entitled *Being Geniuses Together*, Kay Boyle wrote that her visit with Scott in Paris in the fall of 1924 was not an "easy visit" for the following reasons:

> One was aware at every instant of the nervous complexities of Evelyn's marital, and sexual, and professional lives, and in the smoke-filled, crowded hotel room I found it impossible even to hear what was being said. Perhaps I had lived too long in an almost unbroken inner silence, and now in my own confusion and insecurity I trembled for Evelyn's shattered depths. Was she wife, lover, mother, or none of these things, or all of them? It was difficult for me to determine, although all the elements and all the protagonists were there.[7]

Scott and Boyle's friendship lasted until the end of Evelyn's life, but it was a friendship conducted mostly by letters, and Boyle learned much from Scott as a negative example. The pressures that were brought to bear psychologically on Scott as a writer, and as the protagonist in a complex series of layered relationships with (at the time of Boyle's meeting with her in Paris) Cyril Kay-Scott and Owen Merton, in addition to her responsibilities as mother to her son Creighton Scott, were crippling but probably also artistically invigorating. By balancing these roles Scott created energy for her work, but in other ways her practice of always defining herself in terms of others was crippling.

Scott's fragile emotional condition in her later years is graphically suggested by a description of her written by Louise Bogan. In 1955 Scott had approached Bogan, the poetry editor of the *New Yorker*, with a request for advice about her poetry manuscripts. Bogan would have been an important contact for Scott, because she was abreast of trends in poetry, had recently published her collected poems, and had been recognized with the Bollingen Prize for poetry in February of that year. Bogan's response, as reported to May Sarton in a letter of October 1955, reveals a fear of identification with this "mad" woman, as well as exasperation with Scott's manner:

> . . . I had a sad and rather eerie meeting, early this week, with poor old Evelyn Scott. I say *old* advisedly, since she really has fallen into the dark and dank time—the time that I used to fear so much when I was in my thirties. She is old because she has failed to grow—up, in, on. . . . So that at 62 she is not only frayed and dingy (she must have been a beauty in youth) but silly and more than a little mad. She met me only casually, years ago, with Charlotte Wilder, but now, of course, she thinks I can *do* something for her—so transparent, poor thing. She is not only in the physical state I once feared, but she is living in the blighted area of the West 70's, near Broadway: that area which absorbs the queer, the old, the failures, into furnished or hotel rooms, and adds gloom to their decay. It was all there! She took me out to a grubby little tea-room around the corner, insisted on paying for the tea, and brought out, from time to time, from folds in her apparel, manuscripts that will never see print. I never *was* able to read her, even in her hey-day, and her poetry now is perfectly terrible. Added to all this, she is in an active state of paranoia—things and people are her enemies; she has been plotted against in Canada, Hampstead, New York and California; her manuscripts have been stolen, time and time again, etc., etc. —We should thank God, that we remain in our senses! As you know, I really fear mad people; I have some attraction for them, perhaps because talent is a kind of obverse of the medal. I must, therefore detach myself from E. S. I told her to send the MS to Grove Press, and that is all I can do. "But I must know the editor's name!" she cried. "I can't chance having my poems fall into the hands of some secretary. . . ."[8]

In these years, Scott's primary contact in the American publishing scene was William Rose Benét, brother of the poets Stephen and Laura, who was an associate editor for *The Saturday Review of Literature* from 1945 to 1950, and a contributing editor for many years before that. Benét took on a restricted and unofficial role as agent for Scott when in March of 1948 she began sending him poems which he then circulated to poetry reviews such as *The Phoenix*, *Harper's*, and *Tiger's Eye*.[9] She mentioned to him at that time that she had enough poetry for a volume, and in fact the earliest typescripts which contribute to the present edition date from 1948. While *The Saturday Review* eventually took several of Scott's poems, including "To

Artists of Every Land," "Apocrypha," "She Dies," and "Survival," and while Benét conscientiously circulated individual poems to magazines, he balked at the proposition that he read *The Gravestones Wept* entire.[10]

Scott experienced similar difficulties in many quarters trying to get *The Gravestones Wept* considered for publication. In December of 1948, Scott reported in a letter to her friend May Mayers that "since 1945 I have been trying to get Scribner's to read my volume of poems 'The Gravestones Wept,' and save for one occasion, when Max Perkins said, after the publication of novels Scribner's might publish it, its very existence has been ignored; though I haven't sent it elsewhere because [I have] no agent, and because I thought perhaps Max Perkins's advice was good—I don't think so now."[11] On January 8, 1949 Scott mailed *The Gravestones Wept* to Lewis Gannett, a long-time friend and publishing contact. In this letter she gives her reader some idea of the context of the manuscript, her hopes for it, and the scope of the book:

> These are poems accumulated between 1930 and the present and I think them both of intrinsic worth and interesting as I have dated them as a sort of emotional history of the last two decades. And certainly their publication would assist, not hinder, the placing of "Escape into Living," and though I had already asked Bill Benét for publishing suggestions, as he hasn't yet given me any, still if he inclines to read the volume and you think this good, he may yet have the necessary constructive idea. And though I was obliged, because of circulating the original here, to send you a carbon that, like the carbons of "Escape into Living," is faintish, I think it clear enough to be read....[12]

Also on January 8, 1949, Scott wrote to Laura Benét to encourage her to read the poems Scott had sent to Bill Benét the previous summer. In a characteristic marginal note on her own carbon of the letter, Scott remarked in 1953, "They were not read by either, or if read, no comment."[13]

On the British side, Scott inquired of Frank Swinnerton where she might send *The Gravestones Wept*. On his advice, Scott sent the manuscript to Faber & Faber on February 5, 1949, where the poems were politely rejected. Geoffrey Faber cited the decline of the poetry market and previous commitments to writers already appearing with their firm.[14] Among the American firms that considered publication of *The Gravestones Wept* were Harcourt Brace, New Directions, and Yale University Press. While these presses responded politely, there is no evidence that any of them undertook a full reading of the volume.

The poems of *The Gravestones Wept*, like Scott's novels of the 1930s and later, reflect an increasing concern with the relationship between art and politics. In her 1937 "Author's Preface" to *Bread and a Sword*, Scott laments the ways in which art is used to promote politics. She states that in an age which doesn't promote artists or provide their basic needs, they are likely to be desperate and bought or swayed as to their perception of truth. The artist who produces propaganda (and her definition of this term would be broad enough to include any art that has an insincere political dimension) is no longer an authority on his or her own work and becomes, instead, a "technocrat" (xiii), whose function is to promote the state's agenda. There are material rewards for producing art useful for the state. Furthermore, Scott maintains, the machine has become a model by which the success of everything else is measured. Even the pursuit of science has been shaped by commercial concerns such that the "free scope of [scientific] investigations" is curbed to promote profits (xv). Thus, in all realms of knowledge, truth is shaped by economic forces.

In our era, faith itself, according to Scott, has been transferred to machines; those who remain skeptical about the effects of a technological age on human knowledge and perception are, in Scott's view, treated as heretics. Furthermore, machines have reorganized how human beings perceive reality: "not only the ruthlessness of competition, but the steam-roller influence of the machine on our physical equipment, tend to deprive us of data for discrimination. We are losing all capacity for refinement of visual response, our hearing is being dulled as we instinctively protect our nerves from the jangle around us by refusing attention" (xvi). This defensive insensitivity is detrimental to the artist, who depends for his insight on the acuity of his perceptions:

> The functional value of art for the artist is contingent on the degree of such clarifications, which transmute what is of individual origin into what is, not merely morally and occasionally, but aesthetically, and, to all intents and purposes, eternally, a universal. And when those signs of acceptance he so desires are given him from without, the oddity of his temperament ceases to oppress him like some brand of Cain, and he is restored to harmony with surrounding society. Then his idiosyncratic relation with his environment is not a handicap, and his strong egoism, combined with imaginative endowments which will have fostered his insight in directions not commonly explored, may supplement race consciousness, as it could not did his vision of things only duplicate what is popular. (xxiv)

According to Scott, artistic creation demands the full economic, political, and aesthetic freedom of the artist. The value of freely generated art for society is that it represents an unfettered interpretation of truth. Therefore the rights of the artist to interpret the truth must be protected against a majority that is often short-sighted and self-interested.

Scott's explanations of the social and aesthetic theory behind *Bread and a Sword* directly relate to themes she explores in poetic form in *The Gravestones Wept*. A narrative technique that she develops in the novel also appears to have informed her poetic technique. In the novel *Bread and a Sword*, Scott seeks to represent multivocality by a system of italicized and bracketed typefaces which indicate "various facets of personality struggl[ing] against each other for ascendancy" (vii). Italicized speech represents thoughts or ideas that are both associative and resisted by the dominant or surface consciousness. In many of the poems of *The Gravestones Wept*, Scott seeks a similar multivocality through the use of italics to portray the complexity of the emotional reactions and thoughts of her personae.

Due to the length of time Scott worked on it, *The Gravestones Wept* is a work of maturity, long dwelt upon, written with the luxury of time and a careful combing by the artist of nuance and detail. This is a rare situation in Scott's work—she rarely had the time (or the patience, perhaps) to dwell with a work before it went to press. Driven often by economic desperation, but at the same time fiercely intent on maintaining her artistic integrity, she lived out one of her major themes—the dilemma of a serious writer attempting to support a life of art in a world where such work is not necessarily valued. *The Gravestones Wept* is first and foremost a child of this struggle, and in the ways in which it succeeds, it is a triumph over adversity.

The Gravestones Wept is also a Modernist work, like *Precipitations* and *The Winter Alone*. In it, Scott attempts to diagnose and resolve the problem of fragmentation in modern life, whether it be the fragmentation resulting from her life choice to be a writer, the fragmentation of experience that she ascribed to technology, or the fragmentary view of human nature resulting from political totalitarianism. Each section in *The Gravestones Wept* explores aspects of this modern problem and points toward her quest for integration of the extremes of experience.

The texts of *Precipitations* and *The Winter Alone* as here published follow the first editions except for certain author's emendations as indicated in the notes. In *The Winter Alone* and *The Gravestones Wept*, infrequent British spellings used by the author have been regularized to American spellings.

Because *The Gravestones Wept* is previously unpublished, editing procedures for these poems have been more complex. The manuscripts of "The Gravestones Wept" reside in two major collections. The earliest extant typescript and its two carbons are housed at the Harry Ransom Humanities Research Center at the University of Texas at Austin. They are from the year 1948 and were circulated as finished in 1948–49. The remaining eight manuscripts are housed in the Special Collections Library of the University of Tennessee at Knoxville. They can be organized into three groups. The earliest version was typed in 1951; three copies survive, an original and two carbon copies. At the time that Scott completed this version she labeled it "final copy" and placed it into binders that she bought in New York on her way to the Huntington Hartford Foundation in California, where she stayed with John Metcalfe in 1953. The second set of the Tennessee group comprises an original and two carbon copies of the volume as it was typed by Scott in 1956 and 1957. She began typing on August 19, 1956 and finished typing on May 10, 1957. This version includes poems that do not appear in earlier versions because they were written after 1951. The final version of the volume was completed on May 17, 1960, and exists as an original with one carbon. Almost no handwritten alterations are made in this version, which has served as the proof text of this volume.

At the time of Scott's death in 1963, she was survived by her second husband, John Metcalfe, also a writer, and her son and his family, who were living in Canada. A doctoral degree candidate in English at Vanderbilt named Robert L. Welker had completed a landmark dissertation on Scott in 1958, and in 1963 he was an assistant professor at Vanderbilt. He had cultivated a friendship with the authors over the years of his dissertation work, becoming quite close to both Scott and Metcalfe. It was Welker's intention to write a biography of Scott for publication, and with this project in mind, Metcalfe gave him all of the papers in Scott's possession at her death. These papers, which included unpublished manuscripts, carbons of letters she had sent, many letters she had received, family photographs and correspondence, and notes for her last, unfinished novel, were shipped from

New York to Nashville where Welker continued to work at Vanderbilt for a time. Welker brought these papers to his next and final teaching position at The University of Alabama at Huntsville, and he gave them to the University of Tennessee at Knoxville in 1996.

It was also Metcalfe's intention to give Welker a group of papers that the couple had stored in London, in order to unite and complete the collection for the biographer. A large collection of materials which date from before Scott's final return to the United States in 1952 remained behind due to the expense of shipping these materials to the United States. In 1968, Metcalfe and Welker arranged to meet in London for the purpose of making the exchange. Fatefully, during the week of their meeting but before the exchange could actually take place, Metcalfe fell down a flight of stairs, and he died a few days later. The papers remained where they were.

The papers in London that Metcalfe had intended to give to Welker eventually found their way to Paula Scott, surviving spouse of Creighton Scott, Evelyn's only child. Paula Scott became Evelyn Scott's literary executor. These papers, now housed in the Evelyn Scott Collection of the Harry Ransom Humanities Research Center at the University of Texas at Austin, represent material up until her departure from England in 1952; they were papers that she deemed could stay behind when she traveled to the United States and had to make difficult choices about what to bring with her for financial reasons. The Tennessee collection includes the materials that made the journey with her from England, plus the materials she generated after 1952. Scott did bring from England some papers from her early years, including a large group of her mother's letters, her marriage license and divorce papers, and many family photographs: items that, one might assume, had primary sentimental importance to the author. These items are now in Knoxville.

A variorum edition of *The Gravestones Wept,* with a detailed editorial discussion, may be found in the editor's dissertation, *A Critical Edition of* The Gravestones Wept, *by Evelyn Scott, with Commentary and Textual Notes,* University of Tennessee, Knoxville, 1998.

---

1. Robert Welker, "Evelyn Scott: A Literary Biography" (Ph.D. diss., Vanderbilt University, 1958), 149.
2. Mary Wheeling White, *Fighting the Current: The Life and Work of Evelyn Scott* (Baton Rouge: Louisiana State University Press, 1998), 38–62.

3. Padraic Colum, "Two Women Poets," review of *Precipitations*, by Evelyn Scott, *The New Republic* 29 (November 2, 1921): 304–05; Mark Van Doren, "Sapphics," review of *Precipitations*, by Evelyn Scott, *The Nation* 112.2896 (January 5, 1921): 20; Lola Ridge, "Evelyn Scott: An Appreciation," review of *Precipitations*, by Evelyn Scott, *Playboy, a Portfolio of Art and Satire* 7 (1921): 24.

4. "Précis of events to be expanded into a third autobiography," Evelyn Scott Collection, Special Collections Library, University of Tennessee at Knoxville; "Author's Preface," *Bread and a Sword* (New York: Charles Scribner's Sons, 1937), vii–xxxi.

5. "Author's Foreword," in *The Gravestones Wept*, Evelyn Scott Collection, University of Tennessee at Knoxville. Scott included a brief foreword with each of the three copies of the 1948 manuscript of *The Gravestones Wept*. This foreword informed the reader that the poems are arranged according to emotional content, that she assigned dates of composition to them for historical interest, and that the poems with religious content date from a brief period when she was Roman Catholic. The copies of this foreword are at the Humanities Research Center at University of Texas. For the three versions of this foreword, see Appendix A in this edition. Scott included an expanded version of the foreword with the 1951 typescript of *The Gravestones Wept*, which is located in the Evelyn Scott Collection at the University of Tennessee at Knoxville. In addition to facts that she relates in the earlier forewords, Scott goes into great detail to describe events that have seemingly little to do with the poems, but have much to do with her personal obsessions. For this 1951 foreword, see Appendix B in this edition.

6. Scott to Bernice Elliot, 11 September 1949, Evelyn Scott Collection, University of Tennessee at Knoxville.

7. Kay Boyle and Robert McAlmon, *Being Geniuses Together: 1920–1930* (Garden City, New Jersey: Doubleday & Co., 1968).

8. Partially quoted in White 1998, 224. Quoted in full from Louise Bogan to May Sarton, 22 October 1955, in *What the Woman Lived: Selected Letters of Louise Bogan 1920–70*, edited by Ruth Limmer (New York: Harcourt, Brace, Jovanovich, Inc., 1973), 300–01.

9. Evelyn Scott to William Rose Benét, 13 March 1948, Evelyn Scott Collection, University of Tennessee at Knoxville.

10. William Rose Benét to Evelyn Scott, 20 May 1949, Evelyn Scott Collection, University of Tennessee at Knoxville. Benét remarked after several written inquiries by Scott:

> In regard to reading your book of poems: I hate to seem unhelpful or unsympathetic. Certainly I am not the latter, but I also, frankly, feel this. You are an eminent writer fully established. You are also, I believe, a good judge of your own work. I do not think that my opinion upon your book of poems would be of any particular moment, both for that reason and because I now rank as one of the rather passé poets of America. Frankly, I should rather not read your book, because we might disagree upon some points in it and, knowing your intensity, I should not like to enter such a disagreement.

11. Evelyn Scott to May Mayers, 20 December 1948, Evelyn Scott Collection, Special Collections Library, University of Tennessee at Knoxville.

12. Scott to Lewis Gannett, 8 January 1949, Evelyn Scott Collection, Special Collections Library, University of Tennessee at Knoxville.

13. Scott to Laura Benét, 8 January 1949, Evelyn Scott Collection, Special Collections Library, University of Tennessee at Knoxville.

14. Geoffrey Faber to Scott, 10 February 1949, Evelyn Scott Collection, Special Collections Library, University of Tennessee at Knoxville. Among poets on their list in the late forties were Louis MacNeice, Walter De la Mare, and W. H. Auden.

A NOTE ON POEMS WITH RACIAL CONTENT
IN *PRECIPITATIONS*

In a recent lecture, Derek Walcott pointed out that even in masterful works of literature (his example was Conrad's *Heart of Darkness*) there are moments when our present cultural awareness makes us cringe, as we encounter racist attitudes that diminish the text.* The work of criticism is in part to evaluate how deeply racist attitudes affect such texts. In some texts the racist moments may be superficial, as the author is nearly free of racial chauvinism, while other texts are so weighted down with racist attitudes that eventually they will sink from view.

Evelyn Scott's first volume of poetry, *Precipitations*, offers abundant evidence that the author, as a product of the South, was thinking about the causes and effects of racial inequality. Her viewpoint on this subject is generally critical of Southern racism, but in some ways she was reproducing the structures of inequality even as she sought to record and critique. The persona of *Precipitations* is definitely a young white woman who enjoys certain racial privileges. Throughout the book whiteness is celebrated as a positive quality, as white skin is associated with ivory, with the moon, and with a mysterious and poetic quality of peace and the good.

In particular, three poems in *Precipitations* date the book as a product of a certain historical moment and a complex of racial attitudes characteristic of that moment. The first poem with overtly racial content appears in a section entitled "Portraits." In this section, the poet has given herself the latitude to try on different points of view in painting word pictures of people. The poem "Nigger" is written from the point of view or mindset of a white male racist. It is a rather clumsy poem, but it sets up in a bald way the method by which the white male gaze has objectified a black person, to the point of turning him into a caricature of an actor in a minstrel show:

---

* Lecture at Loyola College of Maryland in Baltimore, on April 19, 2004.

NIGGER

Nigger with flat cheeks and swollen purple lips;
Nigger with loose red tongue;
Flat browed nigger,
Your skull peaked at the zenith,
The stretched glistening skin
Covered with tight coiled springs of hair:
I am up here cold.
I am white man.
You are still warm and sweet
With the darkness you were born in.

As twenty-first-century readers, we may be so taken aback by the racist stereotype of the African American that we fail to note the ways in which Scott distances herself from such racist attitudes. For the speaker of the poem is specifically identified as "white man"—not even *a* white man, but white males as a species, who are identified as inhabiting a "cold" space created by their sense of racial superiority. The question is whether the poem's caricature of the Black man is so offensive as to undercut any artistic or political merit the poem might have. I would argue that the poem, like a snapshot of a lynching, offers an honest representation of white racism in the Jim Crow era. For that reason, and however we evaluate the poem as a thing in itself, it maintains a cultural value as a marker of its time. Although both the black man described in the poem and the white speaker are caricatures, I want to give Evelyn Scott some credit for trying to expose white privilege and racial chauvinism. In this project she is in a relatively small company of early-twentieth-century whites. She points out effectively the limitations of the white male gaze and shows the automatic assumptions that the speaker makes about a person that he is utterly unable to see. In typical Scott form, she also highlights an undercurrent of envy in the speaker's racist perspective.

In another section of *Precipitations*, called "Les Malades Des Pays Chauds" (Patients of Hot Countries) (Scott herself was one such patient, when she fell ill after her pregnancy in Brazil) we find "Pride of Race".

PRIDE OF RACE

I saw his young Anglo-Saxon form
In its white sailor clothes

Cleave through the scampering yellow Latin crowd,
As white and clean as the blade of an archangel;
And, as he reeled along, gloriously drunk,
Those little black and gold dung beetles
Seemed to be pushing and racing over his body.

In this poem the speaker identifies with the sailor that she sees in the crowd, as a fellow member of a racial minority. The imagery is of interest because she associates the sailor with the action and intensity of a weapon, and she highlights his whiteness against a backdrop of indistinguishable color. He is granted a human body in the poem, while all others, with the implicit exception of the speaker herself, are relegated to the role of insects. Once again, we are faced with a poem whose overtly racist imagery may overshadow any implied critical subtexts. The poem does illustrate the multiple linguistic levels on which racism acts. Agency is granted solely to the sailor, who is identified according to heritage. He is granted dignity even though he is "gloriously drunk," for his whiteness outweighs any other qualities he may possess. The poem's title suggests that the persona, living in a culture where she feels isolated by her white skin, identifies strongly with the sailor on the basis solely of his skin color, which is amplified further by his white uniform. He is representing not only a culture, but also a system of control and government from which the persona draws strength. There is much to cringe at here, but again Scott's contribution may well be in her honesty and acknowledgement of white privilege.

The third poem with racial content portrays a lynching. It fuses "Down by the Riverside," a Negro spiritual, with a snapshot of the murder of a black man.

DEVIL'S CRADLE

Black man hanged on a silver tree;
(Down by the river,
Slow river,
White breast,
White face with blood on it.)
Black man creaks in the wind,
Knees slack.
Brown poppies, melting in moonlight,
Swerve on glistening stems
Across an endless field

To the music of a blood white face
And a tired little devil child
Rocked to sleep on a rope.

The image of the victim of the lynching as a "tired little devil child" fuses two racist stereotypes: the black man as an irresponsible child, and the black man as inherently evil. The poem also gives credence to the often-cited justification for lynching, for the image of a supernatural white breast and white face with blood on it suggests that the victim may have raped and possibly murdered a white woman. (In this respect the poem may contain an echo of "Strange Fruit," the song immortalized by Billie Holiday.) Yet the interweaving of the lullaby with a graphic image of the results of white violence casts an ironic shadow over the scene: perhaps the references to the white breast and the white face with blood on it (possibly also "blood on the moon") may refer not so much to what the black victim may or may not have done as to the (white) mythology that led to the violence. From this perspective, "the devil's cradle" can be taken as a description of the entire south, where blacks and whites were raised from infancy to reenact these cultural stereotypes.

The three poems here discussed are the only poems in the 1920 collection that are frankly and straightforwardly about race. However, many other poems in *Precipitations* deal indirectly with white privilege. Poem after poem associates whiteness with white women, breasts, and the moon, and all of these are further associated with the good, peace, and introspection. Insofar as the book repeatedly contrasts these "white" qualities to the darkness of night, a racialized subtext runs through the whole of *Precipitations*. In this respect the book taken as a whole may be read as a dissertation on whiteness and white privilege. Yet a second persistent subtext is the speaker's longing for the darkness of death, and the tension between the desires associated with "whiteness" and "blackness" respectively suggests the complexity of Scott's racial attitudes.

THE COLLECTED POEMS OF EVELYN SCOTT

PRECIPITATIONS

(1920)

MANHATTAN

THE UNPEOPLED CITY

MIDNIGHT WORSHIP: BROOKLYN BRIDGE

In the rain
Rows of street lamps are saints in bright garments
That flow long with the bend of knees.
They lift pale heads nimbussed with golden spikes.

Up the lanes of liquid onyx
Toward the high fire-laden altars
Move the saints of Manhattan
In endless pilgrimage to death,
Amidst the asphodel and anemones of dawn.

ASCENSION: AUTUMN DUSK IN CENTRAL PARK

Featureless people glide with dim motion through a quivering blue silver;
Boats merge with the bronze-gold welters about their keels.
The trees float upward in gray and green flames.
Clouds, swans, boats, trees, all gliding up a hillside
After some gray old women who lift their gaunt forms
From falling shrouds of leaves.

Thin fingered twigs clutch darkly at nothing.
Crackling skeletons shine.
Along the smutted horizon of Fifth Avenue
The hooded houses watch heavily
With oily gold eyes.

STARTLED FORESTS: HUDSON RIVER

The thin hill pushes against the mist.
Its fading defiance sounds in the umber and red of autumn leaves.
Like a dead arm around a warm throat
Is the sagging embrace of the river
Laid grayly about the shore.

The train passes.
We emerge from a tunnel into a sky of thin blue morning glories
Where yellow lily bells tinkle down.
The paths run swiftly away under the lamp glow
Like green and blue lizards
Mottled with light.

WINTER STREETS

The stars, escaping,
Evaporate in acrid mists.
The houses, rearing themselves higher,
Assemble among the clouds.
Night blows through me.
I am clear with its bitterness.
I tinkle along brick canyons
Like a crystal leaf.

FEBRUARY SPRINGTIME

The trees hold out pale gilded branches
Stiff and high in the wind.
On the lawns
Patches of gray-lilac snow
Melt in the hollows of the terraces.

The park is an ocean of fawn-colored plush,
Ridged and faded.
Sharp and delicate,
My shadow moves after me on the rumpled grass—
Grass like a pillow worn by a dear head.
Joy!

THE ASSUMPTION OF COLUMBINE

The lights trickle grayly down from the hoary palisades
And drip into the river.
Leaden reflections flow into the water.
Framed in your window,
Your little face glows deceptively
In a rigid ecstasy,
As the wide-winged morning
Folds back the mist.

FROM BROOKLYN

Along the shore
A black net of branches
Tangles the pulpy yellow lamps.
The shell-colored sky is lustrous with the fading sun.
Across the river Manhattan floats—
Dim gardens of fire—
And rushing invisible toward me through the fog,
A hurricane of faces.

SNOW DANCE

Black brooms of trees sweep the sky clean;
Sweep the house fronts,
And leave them bleak in sleep.
High up the empty moon
Spills her vacuity.

I dance.
My long black shadow
Weaves an invisible pattern of pain.
The snow
Is embroidered with my happiness.

POTTER'S FIELD

Golden petals, honey sweet,
Crushed beneath fear-hastened feet . . .

Silver paper lanterns glow and shudder
In flat patterns
On a gray eternal face
Stained with pain.

LIGHTS AT NIGHT

In the city,
Storms of light
Surge against the clouds,
Pushing up the darkness.

In the country,
Is the faint pressure of oil lamps,
That sputter,
Smothered with earth—
Extinguished in silence.

MIDNIGHT

The golden snow of the stars
Drifts in mounds of light,
Melts against the hot sides of the city,
Cool cheek against burning breast,
Cold golden snow,
Falling all night.

CROWDS

SUMMER NIGHT

The bloated moon
Has sickly leaves glistening against her
Like flies on a fat white face.

The thick-witted drunkard on the park bench
Touches a girl's breast
That throbs with its own ruthless and stupid delight.
The new-born child crawls in his mother's filth.
Life, the sleep walker,
Lifts toward the skies
An immense gesture of indecency.

NEW YORK

With huge diaphanous feet,
March the leaden velvet elephants,
Pressing the bodies back into the earth.

SUNSET: BATTERY PARK

From cliffs of houses,
Sunlit windows gaze down upon me
Like undeniable eyes,
Millions of bronze eyes,
Unassailable,
Obliterating all they see:
The warm contiguous crowd in the street below

Chills,
Mists,
Drifts past those hungry eyes of Eternity,
Melts seaward and deathward
To the ocean.

CROWDS

The sky along the street a gauzy yellow:
The narrow lights burn tall in the twilight.

The cool air sags,
Heavy with the thickness of bodies.
I am elated with bodies.
They have stolen me from myself.
I love the way they beat me to life,
Pay me for their cruelties.
In the close intimacy I feel for them
There is the indecency I like.
I belong to them,
To these whom I hate;
And because we can never know each other,
Or be anything to each other,
Though we have been the most,
I sell so much of me that could bring a better price.

RIOTS

As if all the birds rushed up in the air,
Fluttering;
Hoots, calls, cries.
I never knew such a monster even in child dreams.

It grows:
Glass smashed;
Stores shut;
Windows tight closed;
Dull, far-off murmurs of voices.

Blood—
The soft, sticky patter of falling drops in the silence.
Everything inundated.
Faces float off in a red dream.
Still the song of the sweet succulent patter.

Blood—
I think it oozes from my finger tips.
—Or maybe it drips from the brow of Jesus.

THE CITY AT NIGHT

Life wriggles in and out
Through the narrow ways
And circuitous passages:
Something monstrous and horrible,
A passion without any master,
Male sexual fluid trickling through the darkness
And setting fire to whatever it touches.

That is the master
Bestowing a casual caress on a slave.
Quiver under it!

VANITIES

LULLABY

I lean my heart against the soft bosomed night:
A white globed breast,
And warm and silent flowing,
The milk of the moon.

EMBARKATION FOR CYTHERA

Like jellied flowers
My inflated curves
Melt in the peaceful stagnance of the bath.
If I were to die
I would resist the final agony
With only a faint quiver
From my escaping thighs.

CHRISTIAN LUXURIES

The red fountain of shame gushes up from my heart.
I throw back my long hair and the fountain floats it out
Like a fiery fan.
My wide stretched arms are white coral branches.
The liquid shadows seek between my amber breasts.

But the fire is cool.
It cannot burn me.

NARROW FLOWERS

I am a gray lily.
My roots are deep.
I cannot lift my hands
For one thin yellow butterfly.
Yet last night I grew up to a star.
My shade swirled mistily
Seven mountains high.
I lifted my face to another face.
The moon made a burning shadow on my brow.
Washed by the light,
My sharp breasts silvered.
My dance was an arc of mist
From west to east.

EYES

There are arms of ice around me,
And a hand of ice on my heart.
If they should come to bury me
I would not flinch or start.
For eyes are freezing me—
Eyes too cold for hate.
I think the ground,
Because it is dark,
A warmer place to wait.

AFTER YOUTH

Oh, that mysterious singing sadness of youth!
Exotic colors in the lamplit darkness of wet streets,
Musk and roses in the twilight,
The moon in the park like a golden balloon . . .

Then to awaken and find the shadows fled,
The music gone . . .
Empty, bleak!
My soul has grown very small and shriveled in my body.
It no longer looks out.
It rattles around,
And inside my body it begins to look,
Staring all around inside my body,
Like a crab in a crevice,
Staring with bulging eyes
At the strange place in which it finds itself.

THE SHADOW THAT WALKS ALONE

The silence tugs at my breast
With formless lips,
Like a heavy baby,
Attenuates me,
Draws me through myself into it.
I sit in the womb of an idiot,
Helpless before its mouthing tenderness.
The huge flap ears are attentive,
And the soundless face bends toward me
In horrible lovingness.

BIBLE TRUTH

To die . . .
Oh, cool river!
To float there with nothing to resist—

One ripple of silence spreads out from another.
My spirit widens so,

Circle beyond circle.
I hold up the stars no longer with the pupils of my eyes.
Hands, legs, arms float off from me.
I melt like flakes of snow.

I am no more opposed.
I am no more.

THE MATERNAL BREAST

I walked straight and long,
But I never found you.
I was looking for a hill of a hundred breasts,
A hill modeled after the statues of Diana of the Ephesians.
I was looking for a hill of mounds hairy with grass,
And a place to lie down.

AIR FOR G STRINGS

White hands of God
With fingers like strong twigs flowering
Rock me in leaves of iron,
Leaves of blue.

Hands of God
Fashioned of clouds
Have finger tips that balance the almond white moon.
The pale sky is a flower
White tipped and pink tipped with dawn.
White hands of God gather the blossoms with fingers that hold me,
Cloud fingers like milk in the azure night,
Weaving strong chords.

I am lost in the vast cave of night.
No sound but the far-off tinkle of stars,
And the cry of a bird
Muffled in shadows.

The light flows in remotely
Through the hollow moon,
Dim strange brilliance
From waters beyond the sky.
Groping,
I listen to the harsh tinkle of the far-off stars,
Feel the clammy shadows about my shoulders.

THE RED CROSS

HECTIC

Ruby winged pains flash through me,
Jewel winged agonies:
They vanish,
Carrying me with them
Without my knowing it.

II

Pain sends out long tentacles
And sucks.
When I have given up struggling
He takes me into his arms.

ISOLATION WARD

We are the separate centers of consciousness
Of all the universes.
We vibrate statically on a trillion golden wires.
Our trillion golden fingers twine in the weltering darkness,
And grasp tremblingly,
Aware in agony
Of the things we can never know.

THE RED CROSS

Antiseptic smells that corrode the nostrils
Crumble me,
Eat me deep;
And my garments disintegrate:
First my nightgown,
Leaving my naked arms and legs disjointed,
Sprawled about the bed in postures meaningless to the point of
obscenity.

My breasts shrivel,
The nipples drawn like withered plums
To the eyes of the bright young nurse.
I am nothing but a dull eye myself,
An eye out of a socket,
Bursting,
Contorted with hideous wisdom.

Eye to eye
We fight in the death throes,
Myself and the young nurse.
Her firm, crisp aproned bosom
Leans toward the bed,
As she smooths the rumpled pillow back
With long cool fingers.

HOSPITAL NIGHT

I am Will-o'-the-Wisp.
I float in a little pool of delirium,
Phosphorescent velvet.
My fire is like a breath
That blows my illness in circles,
Widening it so far

That I cannot see the edge.
It is one with the night sky.
My fire has blown this vastness,
But I strain and flicker trying to escape from it.
I want to exist without the darkness
That makes my breath so bright.
I want the morning to thin my light.

DOMESTIC CANTICLE

SPRING SONG

Sap crashes suddenly through dead roots:
Sap that bites,
Harsh,
Impatient,
Bitter as gold.

My God, my sisters, how dark, how silent, how heavy is earth!
Shoulders strain against this eternity,
Against the trickling loam.
Earth dropped on the heart like a nerveless hand:
On the red mouth
Earth coils,
Heavy as a serpent.
Light has come back to the darkness,
To the shadow,
To the coolness of blackened leaves.

HOME AGAIN

Where I used to be
I could hear the sea.
The black ragged palm fronds flung themselves against the twilight sky.
The moon stared up from the water like a fish's eye.
I had the loneliness that sings.
It made me light and gave me wings.

Is it the dust and the iron railings and the blank red brick
That makes me sick?

There is no space to be lonely any more
And crumbling feet on a city street
Sound past the door.

TO A SICK CHILD

At the end of the day
The sun rusts.
The street is old and quiet.
The houses are of iron.
The shadows are iron.
Shrill screams of children scrape the iron sky.
Let us lock ourselves in the light.

Let the sun nail us to the hot earth with his spikes of fire,
And perhaps when the darkness rushes past
It will forget us.

LOVE SONG

(TO C. K. S.)

Little father,
Little mother,
Little sister,
Little brother,
Little lover,
How can I go on living
With you away from me?

How can I get up in the morning
And go to bed at night,
And you not here?

How can I bear the sunrise and the sunset,
And the moonrise and the moonset,
And the flowers in the garden?

How can I bear them,
You,
My little father,
Little mother,
Little sister,
Little brother,
Little lover?

QUARREL

Abruptly, from a wall of clear cold silence
Like an icy glass,
Myself looked out at me
And would not let me pass.
I wanted to reach you
Before it was too late;
But my frozen image barred the way
With vacant hate.

MY CHILD

Tentacles thrust imperceptibly into the future
Helplessly sense the fire.
A serpentine nerve
Impelled to lengthen itself generation after generation
Pierces the labyrinth of flames
To rose-colored extinction.

I

I have made you a child in the womb,
Holding you in sweet and final darkness.
All day as I walk out
I carry you about.
I guard you close in secret where
Cold eyed people cannot stare.
I am melted in the warm dear fire,
Lover and mother in the same desire.
Yet I am afraid of your eyes
And their possible surprise.
Would you be angry if I let you know
That I carried you so?

II

I could kiss you to death
Hoping that, your protest obliterated,
You would be
Utterly me.
Yet I know—how well!—
Like a shell,
Hollow and echoing,
Death would be,
With a roar of the past
Like the roar of the sea.
And what is lifeless I cannot kill!
So you would make death work your will.

III

In most intimate touch we meet,
Lip to lip,
Breast to breast,
Sweet.
Suddenly we draw apart
And start.
Like strangers surprised at a road's turning
We see,
I, the naked you;
You, the naked me.
There was something of neither of us
That covered the hours,
And we have only touched each other's bodies
Through veils of flowers.
But let us smile kindly,
Like those already dead,
On the warm flesh
And the marriage bed.

IV

The blanched stars are withered with light.
The moon is pale with trying to remember something.
Light, straining for a stale birth,
Distends the darkness.

I, in the midst of this travail,
Bring forth—
The solitude is so vast
I am glad to be freed of it.
Is it the moon I see there,
Or does my own white face
Hang in blank agony against the sky
As if blinded with giving?

V

Little inexorable lips at my breast
Drink me out of me
In a fine sharp stream.
Little hands tear me apart
To find what they need.

I am weak with love of you,
Little body of hate!

BRUISED SUNLIGHT

WATER MOODS

RAIN ON THE SEASHORE

Curling petals of rain lick silver tongues.
Fluffy spray is blown loosely up between thin silver lips
And slithers, tinkling in hard green ice, down the gray rocks.

White darkness—
An expressionless horizon stares with stone eyes.
The sea lifts its immense self heavily
And falls down in sickly might.

The emptiness is like a death of which no one shall ever know.

SHIP MASTS

They stand
Stark as church spires;
Bare stalks
That will blossom
(Tomorrow perhaps)
Into flowers of the wind.

MONOCHROME

Gray water,
Gray sky drifting down to the sea.
The night,
Old, ugly, and stern,
Lies upon the water,
Quivering in the twilight
Like a tortured belly.

ANTIQUE

Clouds flung back
Make fan-shaped rays of faded crimson
Brocaded on dim blue satin;
Through the wrinkled dust-blue water
The little boat
Glides above its sunken shadow.

ECHO LOOKS AT HERSELF

The ship passes in the night
And drags jagged reflections
Like gilded combs
Through the obscure water.
Spun glass daisies float on a gold-washed mirror.

SPELL

In the dark I can hear the patter.
Bare white feet are running across the water.
White feet as bright as silver

Are flashing under dull blue dresses.
Wet palms beat,
Impatiently,
Petulantly,
Slapping the wet rocks.

RAINY TWILIGHT

Dim gold faces float in the windows.
Dim gold faces and gilded arms . . .

They are clinging along the silver ladders of rain;
They are climbing with ivory lamps held high,
Starry lamps
Over which the silver ladders
Thicken into nets of twilight.

THE STORM

Herds of black elephants,
Rushing over the plains,
Trample the stars.
The ivory tusk of the leader
(Or is it the moon?)
Flashes, and is gone.
Tree tops bend;
Crash;
Fire from hoofs;
And still they rush on,
Trampling the stars,
Bellowing,
Roaring.

NYMPHS

The drift of shadows on the mountainside,
Blue and purple gold!
Purple dust sifting through fingers of ivory:
Cool purple on ivory breasts.
I see arms and breasts,
Upturned chins,
Slanting through the dust of purple leaves:
Ivory and gold,
Bare breasts and laughing eyes,
That drift on the shadowy surf
And surge against the side of the mountain.

WINTER DAWN

Cloudy dawn flower unfolds;
Moon moth gyrates slowly;
Snow maiden lets down her hair,
And in one shining silence,
It slips to earth.

SPRINGTIME TOO SOON

The moon is a cool rose in a blue bowl.
There are no more birds.
The last leaf has fallen.
The trees in the twilight are naked old women.

The moon is an old woman at the door of her tomb.
Clouds combed out in the wind
Are gray hair she has wound about her neck.
The water is an old gray face that mirrors the springtime.

STARS

Like naked maidens
Dancing with no thought of lovers,
Blinking stars with dewy silver breasts
Pass through the darkness.
White and eager,
They glide on
Toward the gray meshed web of dawn
And the mystery of morning.
Then,
About me,
The white cloud walls
Stand as sternly as sepulchers,
And from all sides
Peer and linger the startled faces,
Pale in the harshness of the sunlight.

NIGHT MUSIC

Through the blue water of night
Rises the white bubble of silence—
Rises,
And breaks:
The shivered crystal bell of the moon,
Dying away in star splinters.
The still mists bear the sound
Beyond the horizon.

NOCTURNE OF WATER

A shining bird plunges to the deep,
Becomes entangled with seaweed,
And never more emerges.
Pale golden feathers drift across the sky,
Fire feathered clouds,
Riding the weightless billows of black velvet
On the horizon.

THE LONG MOMENT

A white sigh clouds the fields
Into quietness.
Above the billowed snow
I drift,
One year,
Two years,
Three years.
Hurt eyes mist in the blue behind me.
The moon uncoils in glistening ropes
And I glide downward along the dripping rays
To a marble lake.

DESIGNS

I

Night

Fields of black tulips
And swarms of gold bees
Drinking their bitter honey.

II

New Moon

Above the gnarled old tree
That clings to the bleakest side of the mountain,
A torch of ivory and gold;
And across the sky,
The silver print
Of spirit feet,
Fled from the wonder.

III

Tropic Moon

The glowing anvil,
Beaten by the winds;
Star sparks,
Burning and dying in the heavens;
The furnace glare
Red
On the polished palm leaves.

Winter Moon

A little white thistle moon
Blown over the cold crags and fens:
A little white thistle moon
Blown across the frozen heather.

ARGO

White sails
Unbillowed by any wind,
The moon ship,
Among shoals of cloud,
Stranded stars,
Bare bosoms,
And netted hair of light,
On the shores of the world.

JAPANESE MOON

Thick clustered wistaria clouds,
A young girl moon in a mist of almond flowers,
Boughs and boughs of light;
Then a round-faced ivory lady
Nodding among fading chrysanthemums.

HOT MOON

Moon rise.
Great gong sounds, shining—
Little feet run away.
Loud and solemn, the funeral gong.
Little feet run away.

THE NAIAD

The moon rises,
Glistening,
Naked white,
Out of her stream.

Wet marble shoulders
Shake star drops on the clouds.

FLOODTIDE

Across the shadows of the surf
The lights of the ship
Twinkle despondently.
The clinging absorbent gray darkness
Sucks them into itself:
Drinks the pale golden tears greedily.

Night scatters grapes for the harvest.
The moon burns like a leaf.
Along the mountain path
A thin streak of light
Creeps hungrily with its silver belly to the earth.
The old hound laps up the shadows.
Her teats drip the brighter darkness.

CONTEMPORARIES

HARMONICS

YOUNG MEN

Fauns,
Eternal pagans,
Beautiful and obscene,
Leaping through the street
With a flicker of hoofs,
And a flash of tails,

You want dryads
And they give you prostitutes.

YOUNG GIRLS

Your souls are wet flowers,
Bathed in kisses and blood.
Golden Clyties,
The wheel of light
Rushes over your breasts.

HOUSE SPIRITS

Women are flitting around in their shells.
Pale dilutions of the waters of the world
Come through the windows.

Back and forth the women glide in their little waters;
Cellar to garret and garret to cellar,
Winding in and out under door arches and down passages,
They and their spawn,
In the shell,
In the cavern.

You may come in the shell to overpower her,
Males,
But in the shell, in the shell.
She cannot be torn from the shell without dying;
And what is the pleasure of intercourse with the dead?

AT THE MEETING HOUSE

Souls as dry as autumn leaves,
The color long since out.

The organ plays.
The leaves crackle and rustle a little;
Then sink down.

Old ladies with gray moss on their chins,
Old men with camphor and cotton packed around their heads,
Thin child spirits, sharp and shrill as whistles.

Gray old trees;
Gaunt old woods;
Souls as dry as leaves
After autumn is past.

PURITANS

Blind, they storm up from the pit.
You gave them the force,
You, when You poured the measure of agony into them.
Didn't You know what it would be,
Giving blind people fire?
Not gold and red and amber fire,
But marsh fire.
Fire of ice,
Suffering forged into suffering!

They are coming up now.
The sword is uplifted in the hands of the monster.

My valiant little puppets,
Did you think you could stand out against this?
Pierrot and Columbine bleeding in the flowers. . . .

There must be no flowers.

DEVIL'S CRADLE

Black man hanged on a silver tree;
(Down by the river,
Slow river,
White breast,
White face with blood on it.)
Black man creaks in the wind,
Knees slack.
Brown poppies, melting in moonlight,
Swerve on glistening stems
Across an endless field
To the music of a blood white face
And a tired little devil child
Rocked to sleep on a rope.

WOMEN

Crystal columns,
When they bend they crack;
Brittle souls,
Conforming, yet not conforming—
Mirrors.

Masculine souls pass across the mirrors:
Whirling, gliding ecstasies—
Retreating, retreating,
Dimly, dimly,
Like dreams fading across the mirrors.

Then the mirrors,
Stark and brilliant in the sunshine,
Blank as the desert,
Blank as the Sphinx,
Winking golden eyes in the twinkles of light,
Silent, immutable, vacuous infinity,
Illimitable capacity for absorption,
Absorbing nothing.

Have the shapes and the shadows been swallowed up
In your recesses without depth,
You drinkers of life,
Twinkling maliciously
Your golden yellow eyes,
Mirrors winking in the sunshine?

PENELOPE

Gray old spinners,
Weaving with the crafty fibers of your souls;
Nothing was given you but those impalpable threads.

Yet you have bound the race,
Stranglers,
With your silver spun mysteries.
All the cruel,
All the mad,
The foolish,
And the beautiful, too:
It all belongs to you
Since the first time
That you began to drop the filmy threads
When the world was half asleep.

Sometimes you are young girls;
Sometimes there are roses in your hair.
But I know you—
Sitting back there in the hollow shadows of your wombs.
The crafty fibers of your souls
Are woven in and out
With the fibers of life.

POOR PEOPLE'S DREAMS

Sometimes women with eyes like wet green berries
Glide across the slick mirror of their own smiles
And vanish through lengths of gold and marble drawing rooms.
The marble smiles,
As sensuous as snow;
Hips of the Graces;
Shoulders of Clytie;
Breasts frozen as foam,
Frozen as camelia bloom;
Mounds of marble flesh,
Inexplicable wonder of white . . .

I dream about statuesque beauties
Who look from the shadows of opera boxes;
Or elegant ladies in novels of eighteen thirty,
At the hunt ball . . .
Reflections in a polished floor,
A portrait by Renoir,
A Degas dancing girl,
English country houses,
An autumn afternoon in the Bois,
Something I have read of . . .
In sleep one vision retreating through another,
Like mirrors being doors to other mirrors,
Satin, and lace, and white shoulders,
And elegant ladies,
Dancing, dancing.

FOR WIVES AND MISTRESSES

Death,
Being a woman,
Being passive like all final things,
Being a mother,
Waits.

Shining faces
Gray and melt into her flesh.
Death envies those asleep in her,
Little children who have come back,
Fiery faces,
Bright for a moment in the darkness,
Extinguished softly in her womb.

PORTRAIT OF RICH OLD LADY

Old lady talks,
Spins from her lips
Warp and woof
Of teapots, tables, napery,
Sanitary toilets,
Old bedsteads, pictures on walls,
And fine lace,
Spins a cocoon of this secondary life.

Warm and snug in old lady's belly,
Old lady makes Venus Aphrodite
Parvenue.
Old lady
Arranges places for courtesans
In warm outbuildings on back streets.

NIGGER

Nigger with flat cheeks and swollen purple lips;
Nigger with loose red tongue;
Flat browed nigger,
Your skull peaked at the zenith,
The stretched glistening skin
Covered with tight coiled springs of hair:
I am up here cold.
I am white man.
You are still warm and sweet
With the darkness you were born in.

THE MAIDEN MOTHER

He has a squat body,
Glowering brows,
And bulging eyes.
Lustful contemplation of the meat pie
Is written all over his sweating face.

The thin woman with the meek voice,
Who has carried him so long in her body
And despairs of giving him birth,
Watches over him in secret
With bitter and resentful tenderness.

A PIOUS WOMAN

You can bury your face in her thick soul of cotton batting
And smell candle wax and church incense.
When she dies she must be burned.
Laid in the ground she would only soak up moisture
And get soggy,
As now she has a way of soaking up tears
Never meant for her.

A VERY OLD ROSE JAR

She ran across the lawn after the cat
And I saw through the old maid, as through a shadow,
A young girl in a white muslin dress running to meet her lover.
There was clashing of cymbals,
And the flash of nereids' arms in autumn leaves.
A sharp high note died out like an ascending light.
Something sweet and wanton faded from the old maid's lips—

Something of Pierrot chasing after love,
A bacchante dying in her sleep,
A shadow,
And a gray cat.

THE NIXIE

He lies in cool shadows safe under rocks,
His eyes brown stones,
Worn smooth and soft,
But uncrumbled.
He reaches forth covert child-claws
To tickle the silver bellies of the little blind fish
As they swim secretly above him.
He laughs—
The school splinters, panic stricken.

As we stare through the lucid gold water
He gazes up at us from his shadowy retreat
In combative safety.
There are times when he pretends to himself that he is a god,
Water god, land god, god-in-the-sky.
We cannot laugh at his grotesquerie.
We are wistful before the pathetic gallantries of his imagination.

OLD LADIES' VALHALLA

I am thinking of a little house,
A pretty gray silk dress,
And a little maid with a tidy white apron.

I am thinking of thin yellow angels
Flying out of Sèvres china tea cups,

And a cool spirit with slanting green eyes,
Who peers at me through the screen of plants
I have placed in the corner between the hearth and the window.
I am thinking of the peace in one's own little home
When the afternoon sunshine drips on the shiny floor,
And the rugs are in order,
And the roses in the bowl plunge into shadow
Like pink nymphs into a pool,
While there is no sound to be heard above the hum of the teaket-
tle
Save the benevolent buzzing of flies in the clean sash curtain.

PORTRAITS OF POETS

I

(FOR L. R.)

To rush over dark waters,
A swift bird with cruel talons;
To seize life—
Your life for hers—
To hold it,
Hold it struggling—
To kiss it.

II

Crystal self-containment,
Giving out only what is sent.
Startled,
The circumference retreats
As it mounts higher, flamelike,
Still and clear without radiance,

Ascending without self-explanation.
A skeleton falls apart
With the dignity of comprehensible pathos,
The bones bleached by denial.

III

With the impalpable lightness of May breezes
Begins a battle of flower petals:
Cowering in the primrose whirlwind his lips have blown,
The little grotesque with the shattered heart,
Fearful,
Yet sinister in his fearfulness.

THEODORE DREISER

The man body jumbled out of the earth, half formed,
Clay on the feet,
Heavy with the lingering might of chaos.
The man face so high above the feet
As if lonesome for them like a child.
The veins that beat heavily with the music they but half under-
stood
Coil languidly around the heart
And lave it in the death stream
Of a grand impersonal benignance.

PIETÀ

The child—
Warm chubby thighs,
Fat brown arms,
An unsurprised face—

Cries for jam.
The mother buys him with jam.
An old woman,
Tottering on lean leather skinned legs,
Sucks with glazing eyes
The crystal silken milk
That flows from the death wound
In a young flower-soft, jewel-soft body.

BRAZIL THROUGH A MIST

THE RANCH

TROPICAL LIFE

White flower,
Your petals float away
But I hardly hear them.

TWENTY-FOUR HOURS

The day is so long and white,
A road all dust,
Smooth monotony;
And the night at the end,
A hill to be climbed,
Slowly, laboriously,
While the stars prick our hands
Like thistles.

RAINY SEASON

A flock of parakeets
Hurled itself through the mist;
Harsh wild green
And clamor-tongued
Through the dim white forest.
They vanished,

And the lips of Silence
Sucked at the roots of Life.

MAIL ON THE RANCH

The old man on the mule
Opens the worn saddle bags,
And takes out the papers.

From the outer world
The thoughts come stabbing,
To taunt, baffle, and stir me to revolt.
I beat against the sky,
Against the winds of the mountain,
But my cries, grown thin in all this space,
Are diluted with emptiness . . .
Like the air,
Thin and wide,
Touching everything,
Touching nothing.

THE VAMPIRE BAT

What was it that came out of the night?
What was it that went away in the night?
The little brown hen is huddled in the fence corner,
Eyes already glazing.
How should she know what came out of the night,
Or what was taken away in the night?
A shadow passed across the moon.
The wind rustled in the mango trees.
And now, in the morning,
The little brown hen is huddled in the fence corner,

Eyes already glazing;
Because a shadow passed across the moon,
And the wind rustled in the mango trees.

CONSERVATISM

The turkeys,
Like hoop-skirted old ladies
Out walking,
Display their solemn propriety.

A terrible force,
Hungry and destructive,
Emanates from their mistily blinking eyes.

LITTLE PIGS

Little tail quivering,
Wrinkled snout thrusting up the mud:
He will find God
If he keeps on like that.

THE SILLY EWE

The silly ewe comes smelling up to me.
Her tail wriggles without hinges,
Both ends of it at once and equal.
Yesterday the parrot bit her;
Last week the jaguar ate her young one;
But experience teaches her nothing.

THE SNAKE

The chickens are at home in the barnyard,
The pigs in the swill,
And the flowers in the garden;
But where do you belong,
With your lacquered coils,
O snake?

THE YEAR

Days and days float by.
On the sides of the mountains
Blue shadows shift
And sift into silence.

Morning ...
The cock crows.
There is that rosy glow on the mountain's edge;
José in the door of his hut;
Maria's lace bobbins
Tapping, tapping.
Evening ...
The parrot's shrill cry;
Pale silver green stars.
Night ...
The ghosts of dead Josés
And dead Marias
Sitting in the moonlight.
Peace—
Depressing,
Interminable
Peace.

BURNING MOUNTAINS

I

A herder set fire to the grass
On the other side of the valley,
And now a beautiful Indian woman
Bends, whirls, undulates,
Tosses her gold braceleted arms into the air—
Then sinks into her gray veil.

II

Fire, dying in smoke,
You stir behind the haze
Like a warrior
Who threatens in his sleep.

VILLA NOVA DA SERRA

The mountains are as dull and sodden
As drunkards' faces,
And the white forgetfulness of rain
Is like a delirium.
Along the filthy crooked streets of the little town,
Street lamps float in pools of mist—
The eyes of children being beaten.

RAIN IN THE MOUNTAINS

Like inexorable peace,
The mists march through the mountains.

One by one the grim peaks sink into the cold arms of the unspoken.
The little town with the pink and white houses
Looses its hold on the ridge of hills
And floats among cloud tops.
A shaggy donkey, cropping grass in the sequestered church yard,
Walks, with a leisurely air,
Into a wind driven abyss.

TROPICAL WINTER

The afternoon is frozen with memories,
Radiant as ice.
The sun sets amidst the agued trembling of the leaves,
Sinking right down through the gold air
Into the arms of the sea.
The enameled wings of the palm trees
Keep shivering, shivering,
Beating the gold air thin. . . .

TALK ON THE RANCH

It is cold in the circle of mountains,
A fireless hearth.
The stars drift by like autumn leaves.
Only the rustle—
Then, close together,
Our talk,
For and counter,
One grating against the other,
Rubs a little fire
And we warm each other
There in the midst of the hollow clammy circle.

PRIDE OF RACE

I saw his young Anglo-Saxon form
In its white sailor clothes
Cleave through the scampering yellow Latin crowd,
As white and clean as the blade of an archangel;
And, as he reeled along, gloriously drunk,
Those little black and gold dung beetles
Seemed to be pushing and racing over his body.

DON QUIXOTE SOJOURNS IN RIO DE JANEIRO

White roses climb the wall of night.
A pale face looks from a window in the sky.
O Moon, is it because you have seen her that you are beautiful?
Is she happy among the saints?
I placed white flowers in the coffin.
Are they the blossoms that lie scattered along the horizon,
Tangled in your light?
Dim stars drop into the sea.
So you give my flowers back to me, do you, Bella Dona?
I might gather the petals and carry them to Antonietta to trim her
hats.
So much for life with a little negro milliner
In the Rua Chile!

CONVENT MUSINGS

Eleven thousand white-faced virgins in the sky.
The eyes of Our Lady
Smiling through a rift of cloud.
I see Sister Maria da Gloria's fat shadow
Pass across the whitewashed wall by the window. . . .

Eleven thousand white-faced virgins—
Stars from a broken rosary—
The Southern Cross—
Thrum, thrum, my fingers on the bench.
I sometimes think of God
As an enormous emptiness
Into which we must all enter at last,
Our Lady forgive me.

GUITARRA

"An orange tree without fruit,
So am I without loves,"
His heavy lidded eyes sang up to her.

Her glance dropped on her golden globe of breast,
And on the baby.

Foreign sailors in the streets
Are as sad a sight as wild geese in the winter—

There was one boy with those strange young blue eyes
Who looked at me;
And a long, long time after he had passed
The light of his soul got to me—
So long on the way—
Like the light of a dead star.

What makes you look so lonesome, Blue Eyes?

THE COMING OF CHRIST

THE DEATH OF COLUMBINE

DUET

Pierrot sings.
The moon, a clown like himself,
Stares down upon him
With vacuous tenderness.
For a moment the night is filled with rice powder
And spangled gauze.
Then two shades embracing each other
Find in their arms
Only the darkness.

FROM A MAN DYING ON A CROSS

The pains in my palms are threads of sightless fire
Drawn like fiery veins through blackened marble walls,
Crashing with a dull roar
To the ends of the earth.

Winey peace. . . .
My sick blood purrs.
Milky bosoms float through red hair,
Gaunt faces and sick eyes
Beside her face.
I debauch them with my forgiveness.
Only her, I cannot forgive.

Moonlight trembles as the silk of her garment,
Perfumed silk.
The cross makes a long harsh shadow
Rigid on the sand.
Her white feet stir across the shadow.

LAGNIAPPE

You in the quiet garden,
You with the death sweet smile,
Before you speak of love to me
Go out and hate awhile.

The kind devil
Has a tolerant grin.
He flings the golden gates out wide
And lets poor people in.
He warms them in his bosom
And guards their pain.
He shows them hell fields that are bright
And skies gentle with rain.
But up in paradise
The stern Lord is wise,
And Michael with his flaming sword
Puts out the angels' eyes.

HAIL MARY!

Pierrette is dead!
Between her narrow little breasts
They have laid a cross of lead.
Her tight pale lips are sunken.
Her fleshless fingers clutch the pall.

Why did she have to die like that,
And she so small?

THE DEATH OF COLUMBINE

White breast beaten in sea waves,
Hair tangled in foam,
Lonely sky,
Desolate horizon,
Pale and shining clouds:
All this desolate and shining sea is no place for you,
My dead Columbine.

And the waves will bite your breast;
And the wind, that does not know death from life,
Will leap upon you and leer into your eyes
And suck at your dead lips.

Oh, my little Columbine,
You go farther and farther away from me,
Out where there are no ships
And the solemn clouds
Soar across the somber horizon.

PIERROT LAUGHS

You are old, Pierrot,
But I do not laugh
As in harlequinade
You totter down the path.
Now you are old, Pierrot,
And drool to your guitar,
I do not cast you off.

Though your love songs are as feeble as a winter fly's
I do not scoff.
Exultant
I cast back on you
What you gave me,
And bind you with the unasked love
That has kept me from being free!

THE TRANSMIGRATION OF CALIBAN

Once I had a little brother,
An ugly little brother that was I.
I was still in the nursery
When they nailed him to a clean white cross,
And said he was dead.
He flapped there all day,
Thin and stiff as a jumping jack.

But when I had gone to bed,
And the lights were out,
And the muslin curtains rustled in white secrecy,
And through the thin brown glass like onion skin
I could see the bright moon sag to the tree tops
With a heaviness I dimly understood,
While the haggard branches gauntly strained,
As useless to the moon as she to them,
I was rocked in an orange and umber cradle,
A rosy bubble alight with fireshine
Floating atop the cold,
And my little brother was burning merrily,
His twisted figure
A writhing grotesque.

Yet his face never moved
And never burnt up.
And when I had drifted asleep

I still saw it
Like a reflection trapped in a mirror.
And I couldn't brush it out!
I couldn't brush it out!

GUNDRY

There are little blood flecks on the snow.
There is blood in the heart of the white hyacinth.
I saw her pale body harsh as a flash of lightning
Between the gray torsos of the trees.
She had a little child.
She held a little child in her breast.
She went quickly through the dim forest.
I have seen her feet.
They are as white as ivory.
Where she ran there are little red tracks.
And it is not yet springtime!

VIENNESE WALTZ

Dresden china shepherdesses
Whirl in the silver sunshine:
Columbine stars
Float in gauze petticoats of light. . . .
Little Columbine ghosts, wrinkled and old,
Smelling of jasmine and camphor:
Prim arms folded over immaculate breasts. . . .

The pirouetting tune dies. . . .
Stars and little faded faces,
Waltzing, waltzing,
Shoot slowly downward

On tinkling music,
Dusty little flowers
Sinking into oblivion.

After the music,
Quiet,
The glacial period renewed,
Monsters on earth,
A mad conflagration of worlds on ardent nights—

These too vanishing—
Silence unending.

RESURRECTION

IMMORTALITY

Death is a child of stone.
Death is a little white stone goat.
The little goat child dances motionless.
Little kid feet make a circle around the world:
Bas-relief of Death,
Little stone goats capering across the clouds.

Perhaps Death is nearest in the spring.
Then Her flower clouds the woods with white blossoms,
Apple blossoms, quince blossoms,
Pear snow.
These are the flowers that drift in the hair of the dead.
The sun shines on stone eyelids
That melt with light.
This smile is a pale happiness;
It glows motionless
On the rocky hillside and the long stems of trees.
There are no shadows in this happy light:
The glow beat by little goat hoofs
Chiseled across the clouds in motionless delight,
While suns fade behind crumbling hillsides
And hungry illusions vanish
In generation after generation.

AUTUMN NIGHT

The moon is as complacent as a frog.
She sits in the sky like a blind white stone,
And does not even see Love
As she caresses his face with her contemptuous light.

She reaches her long white shivering fingers
Into the bowels of men.
Her tender superfluous probing into all that pollutes
Is like the immodesty of the mad.
She is a mad woman holding up her dress
So that her white belly shines.
Haughty,
Impregnable,
Ridiculous,
Silent and white as a debauched queen,
Her ecstasy is that of a cold and sensual child.

She is Death enjoying Life,
Innocently,
Lasciviously.

VENUS' FLY TRAP

A wax bubble moon trembles on the honey-blue horizon.
Softly heated by your breast
Pearl wax languorously unfolds her lily lips of mist,
Swells about you,
Weaves you into herself through each moist pore,
Absorbs you deliciously,
Destroys you.

SUICIDE

A dirty little beetle
Peers into motionless eyes
Transfixed to their depths
As by shining needles.
Limbs are taut in ultimate resentment.

A bare sky confronts an upturned face.
Like a wheel vanishing in speed
The corpse, containing everything,
Has swallowed itself.

LEAVES

I

The women hold a child up for a shield,
And speak of it tenderly,
Seeing it bloody.

II

The lovers throw back the scented coverlet
And are afraid.
Seeing Death in their own nakedness,
They shroud it with flowers.

III

The corpse was stiff like an arrow.
As they carried it past the onlookers
It pierced the crowd with its life.
Blank white faces floated back
In terror of its vividness.

IV

The man was dead.
It was seen to that he was buried.

Again and again they dug the bones up,
But when they could no longer find the bones
They groped for the proof of death
In fear of the resurrection.

ALLEGRO

(At the Cemetery)

The mounds stir in the sunshine.
Bones clack a light staccato.
Bare wrist bones,
Thigh bones,
Ankle bones,
Kick the soil loose.

Moldy draperies flutter back and forth through the light.
The trees have put on a thin green pretense.
Even the soil pretends to fecundity.
Toothless jaws widen in a smile of real mirth.
Bones lightened of flesh
Flash in the sunshine.

And afterward
The dead rest in the spring night,
Each in a silence molded to him,
Each in his own night,
A casket with a spangled lining.
The dead rest deep in their happiness.

THE WINTER ALONE

(1930)

BRIGHT WORLD

EARLY SPRING DAY

How thin and meager joy,
Wasted by the long effort of the winter,
By too much sleep!
Apple trees have risen with blossoms,
Pale yet with the dream.
Clover is reluctant.
Dandelions tighten to the jostle of the wind.
A butterfly is lost.
The leaves look young.
The sound they make
Recalls a sorrow that is old,
A whisper as of tears
Sweetened after a long time.
People in the fields are toiling heavily
To bring forth all the springs they have remembered.

MEMORIES OF A SEASON

I

Under the thistledown craigs,
The white ramparts of heaven,
In blue too pure to be answered by anything but tears,
In glistered twilight,
Dolphin waters stride along the beach,
Striking from the sands
A miracle of fog-pale crests.
Winds stridulate.
The one star flake,

Stainless to the mists,
Trembles . . .

A moon,
Lean as tallow,
Strokes with lightning
Each pondered wave,
Flattering space with such motion
As angels might use to embrace the earth;
While there pours over,
Between me and the sunken flame,
A torrent clear as burning honey.

II

On days
When the dead confusion of other people's thoughts
Clutters an alive mind,
One meditates
As in the debris of an autumn forest.
For even the tiniest flash of emerald from the deep mould,
Be grateful!

But when,
Along the front at evening,
I evade the paralytic tentacles of pier,
Where waves steam in their limp descent
On agate murk of shingle,
And boats,
Bannered in lamps—
The miracles of children—
The stern moon presses me.
My life rises with her,
Tingling,
To meet her nacreous life.

The moon,
Bleak and thoughtful on the dark water,
Scalds with milk
Beaches, heavy, urgent waves,
Each swollen to meet its time,
Not one before the hour.
Over the death-rattle of shingle,
Out of platinum caves,
Mercurial curlings about submerged rocks,
The august fountains of the spume
Leap to fringe heaven.
White violence streams from the shadow.
A black mirror is breathed on
By disaster grown immeasurable.
In the preying midnight
Towers of sleep rise.
Stone-locked serpents hiss.
Under an immense gossamer,
Worlds are stirring;
Desert pricks of stars
Seeding a waste.

I am old tonight.
I listen to the mummy sounds.

LOW TIDE

The blackened rocks
Flaunt emerald manes.
Groynes are our mammoth skeletons
With ribs of lime.
There are pubic mats of seaweed
On the sea wall's slime.

Starfish,
On petalled, furry feet,
Tread ghostly in the pools.
The baby fish,
Through midnight blue,
Swim round in silver schools.
The families
Of limpets
Parade in Chinese hats
Pitch nomad tents
Of pink and tan
'Midst herds of crabs
And rats.
The apple of the moon
Hangs high
In the fever green
And dew.
The water wastes
Are slatey plaques.
It's a world that smells of rue.

SOLITUDE

The sumptuous evening,
With its spires of hemlock
Ragged with dark,
Is an ebony cathedral.
Mountains sink away
Under tides of too much blue.
Air, aching in the nostrils,
Is frozen honey.
The lone tree in the field,
Tortured by her hunted leaves,
Trembles,
Decks in her grey bridal.

Stars are mere mutterings of light
Over the dazed grass.
No lover comes for the cold tree.
The night wind beats her
With its icy whips.
The hour is sweetly poisoned
With the tang of sleep
Grown too inevitable.

LANDSCAPE FOR A PAINTER

Land, roll onward
To confront assembling storms;
Greet, with the blanching of a hundred miles of foliage,
The multiple, lean tremor of bright rain;
Swell and reform
The ecstasy of cataleptic rhythm
The eye seeks to recapture,
Until the burden of your calm,
The rearing brilliance of your insult to the sky,
Is human pain!

DEFIANCE TO GREY SPRING

The grey spring hangs above us.
The houses open all their dark and empty windows.
Yet nature does not love us.
The rain is chill as bitter poison
In the silver air.
It teases all the little sodden hummocks in the gardens.
It will not leave them in the peace wherein it found them.
It will not leave the patient trees that stood through winter
Reserved and bare.
Invisible across the hanging twilight

The lilac scent drags like a sea,
The perfume flooding us in tides of restlessness,
In precious agony.
I know that I must hunger with the seasons,
Flame with the passive vegetation,
Wither in the winter,
Finally die.
Yet will I speak with language of a thing of mind
And the unbroken will of man,
Though I lie!

SEA AFTERNOON

In the evening
Comes a fierce dove-movement
For the water,
Beating gently on the drunken beaches
An enormous wing,
Scattering white feathers.
The scurfed sands,
In salty glitter,
Are drenched with mildness,
With the tears of the just.
This smells of freedom!

SHIPS IN PORT

Out beyond Sandy Hook,
Beyond anywhere,
Footless caravans are creeping in
On the moving desert.
Along the farthest blue rim of the world
Lines of black camels hump themselves,
Lift fleecy backs, and stagger . . .

It is to the lean, horn-bright voices of my sirens
That I listen.
They are calling from the quays.
Whistles storm against space.
Clouds are flags.
The bleak, immobile eyes of oracle
Flash, jaunty, on the twilight sky.
Vultures for the stale air of ports,
Verminous with men,
My ships are as clean to the wind
As the immortals.
Above the jostling shadows of rootless trees,
They have carved,
In polar rainfall under moons,
Wounds vanishing in beauty:
Bare poems,
In milk, ice, diamonds, steel, cerulean . . .
From the hot, pent city,
Where the people are like frogs in drought,
Maybe an etiolated thought will follow
The reserved trails leading outward,
To lose them forever, with the gulls,
At the first stilted buoy.

SPRING TORMENT

We do not have to look into the florists' shops
To say: It is spring today. Let us go away
Where spring will not be strange;
Though poison run in the black vines,
And the cold creeper, bare as a snake.
The dogwood leaps
With bleakest cries of beauty from the mould,
In the smoke-coloured woods.
Let us go further yet and find
The shell-white rind that halts the spray;

To a never-end where we need no friend:
Where boat sails dip and flap and beat,
In the dazzle of the sleet.
We stare into a florist's shop.
The raindrops hop from foam-fringed eaves
And slip between us and the lights and leaves.
Above the roofs, under the ramp of heaven,
The storm and winds sough on.
Our hearts are very still. It is spring.
We are ill. We cannot sing.
We wonder what this year will bring.

TANTALIZATION IN REST

The wicked trees at evening
Hang on the verge
In graven obloquy.
A slit of rage is in the all-pervading grey.
The ponds wither,
Wind dwindled,
Where heaven,
Hell-pink and dappled,
Floats upside down.
Cows on a hillside are rooted in the dim.
Only their necks,
Flat-turned on the low light,
Swerve occasionally
To make a nimble garden.

My dry and peaceful heart
Looks chillily at twilight—
At the wine and the rose,
The seething and temptation.
Indifference—
Or is this happiness?

The furred, brown trees,
On the grey sky,
Suggest frail patterns on the wings of moths.
An ivory dew is in the air.
The soundless dray horse wears a silver comb.
There are the mouse-steps of the passersby
Across the silvery ash.
The world is morbid sculpture that was moulded
In a lightning flash.
There are infant garlands on the rosebushes.
Surely the great elms are a young orchard.
The giants are like stalks of wintry fern.
As if the leaves grew feathers,
Down clings, and to the very icicles.
Among the wool catkins I walk,
Eyes fringed with the torn white flesh,
With crystal.
In the park,
The forests spread the tattered, frosty wings of angels,
Bleached in great fans,
The dead coral.
At evening,
There is a paper universe,
In which nothing lives but a bluish shadow.
Under the arc lamps
The gradual flood descends steadily
Its rainbow particles.
To this core,
All accumulating darkness pivots,
Quickens with infinity . . .
There is silence.

Little white lambs wander
In the bleating air,
Among dark cypresses.
Sirens, far away on the river,
Sometimes repeat
The mournful bleat.
Little lambs stagger under all the sins
Of people living anywhere between The Temple
And Nottinghill Gate,
And much farther.
More and more chill,
More and more melancholy,
Weaker and weaker,
The whistles blearing
All the world of hearing.
Traffic is stopped
Because of the press,
The reckless, woolly guilelessness.
A lamb has died.
The feeble blanching has begun to lift.
But there's still a halo shining
Where mire-stained creatures have squatted
With knees flexed under bleeding bosoms.
There are no trams, no taxis and no buses.
There is no tread of passerby.
Just small, trembling, anaemic ghosts
That stumble on
Through a city hushed
For a lamb to die.

IN SPAIN

At evening,
Before the monastery gates,
When velvet silence,
Poured from brimming valleys,
Dims,
Life ripens from the solitude.
Blue-smocked figures of men
Cluster like grapes . . .
Discussing figures of autumn.
The clock tolls in the bell-tower,
With a tinny and enormous sound,
Wide and mild above the drip of sheep bells
On the roads below.

THE SPLENDID SKY

From the apple-pink east,
To the west, and the cloudy forests of the rain,
Was ten centuries.
From the circle scurfed with mist
Where the sun,
Looking at tomorrow,
Saw its own reflection,
Was another ten centuries.
There is a sea that is nine-hundred fathoms deep;
But the blue in the zenith
Took a million years to make.
It was filled with such redolence of winds
As have blown from polar bitterness to polar bitterness
Through human time.
Tattered lace hurricanes rested over all the lakes of the globe,
In crimson frost, nightmare purple.
Even birds,

Twitching by,
Very high up,
Seemed to take their way
Like tiny boats,
Knowing very little about the Elysian Fields,
The ruin of fire and glass,
The millennium promised
Out of blazing indigo
And welts rosy as sores.

Expanses dwindled.
Under the embankment,
Trains, milking the fog,
Steamed by slowly.
Unmindful of the fifty-thousand molten rose petals
Scorching heaven,
Little boys,
On a grass common,
Where the green was fresh as cinnamon,
Shouted,
Played cricket.
Everything under the sky was very homely.
Nothing seemed to last long.

I have said to myself:
Death haunts me.
Now, gazing at the precious signs,
And again finding beauty so much more than I can bear,
Life haunts me.

OLD HOUSE IN THE SNOW

In the fence corner,
The white, unbended burden
Shows glassy hollows—

Footprints of someone forgotten.
Wistful trees,
Immaculately shorn of leaves,
Drink from the sky
The tingling dark, as it approaches,
Sharpening their pronged boughs.
In eighteen-eighty
Somebody lived here.
Nobody has cared, since,
To sweep the snow away.

THREATENING SUMMER NIGHT

Darkness is heavy
On the close ground.
Lightnings flitter
Without any sound,
The lamps in houses
Far and dim
Along the rim
Of fields in solitude.
Then the world rocks
To velvet shocks,
Deep and reverberant.
The wetted, twitching branches part,
And silver fields blow wide
In all their ashy weeds and flowers,
As night is whetted
By the fragilely imparted rain.
In a mute yielding,
The vaguely expanding earth,
While rippled by an agony as mute,
Gives birth
To something bright and strange,
More utter than the storm;

In that caress of unimpassioned wind,
The trillion seeds of generations sown,
The future that the centuries cannot rescind.

EARLY MORNING

(Béziers)

The fog clings
In the spars of lamps
In the morning damps.
With golden petals
On tall, black stems growing,
The lights are glowing.
Tattered hummocks are the bushes.
Trees have wet and blackened leaves
The wind heaves.
Strange human forms
Pass,
Obsolete,
On tapping feet.
Paler and paler,
Shining on us below,
The moon,
Drifted against a chimney pot,
Is a clot of snow.
The strewn seeds
Of ruddy poppies lying,
The signs across
The boulevard
Are dying.
A brazen fist crashes out of the sky.
In trillion fragments
Glass puddles lie!

REQUIEM

(Béziers)

Strong men's voices make stern joy in the rainy morning.
Under the cross rigid with direction,
Processional surplices swing.
On the rocking show of the feathered hearse,
Bulky with pomp,
On stale mourners, black-drifted, cluttered in the street,
The Bell,
Tolling,
Globular,
Sheds a long sound.
And the heaviness of the drops of sorrow, impersonal,
Melts deathward,
Drifts earth, sky, city and solemn, empty morning
Into the forever and ever—
—*ding-dong, ding-dong*—
Peacefully,
With a vast weight,
Colder than the odor of the flowers.

TRAIN LEAVING

The coach thumped
Upon a steady pulse.
Aloof, long flocks
Of trees
Flung far across
The streaming dusk,
The winter's fripperies.
Birds meandered over
In a desert gloom.
Processional

The fence posts started
Travelling toward the moon.
Chickens in a farmer's run
Were flakes of the vanished light.
Land showed itself
By a hedge, a barn, a roof
That scarred the night.
Smoke
Was a savage intimation
Flooding at our heel.
It swam upon the swarthy lamps
And made the windows reel.
When the last blanched clouds
Swept solemnly behind us
On their passage
Toward the west,
And cold day bore
Into its lake of gore
An arrow pierced my breast.

VOYAGE

I

Upright and proud and isolate
The mast; already past the slow land.
Gulls cleave the sky
Into clean remnants of a lost earth motion;
The hooting gulls
That are the carrion angels of the ocean;
The slow gulls who write themselves severely
On the sinking glare,
Turning their pale heads between
Phantom-feathered shoulders and observing
All light-ships crash away, extinct.

A thin tincture, a small essence that is star,
Hangs over blue and night-charred waters
As they slope and curve and smite
With heavier bludgeoning
The ruddy orchards of the west.
I am alone, and blest.

II

Moon, fine as a shrill whip,
Lashes the clouds,
Shreds gloomy gold
From bitter tendril curled,
Excites a sodden world
To long, colossal tremors.
I feel the oceans sway with me
And all the giddy universe of stars
Beats vastly,
Like the gale-flapped banner
Of a warrior god.

III

Over the numb edge of sky
Climb the snow-travelling mountains,
Vapor fuming,
In ice-grey, running hummocks,
Until the moving Andes has turned white with gale.
Jade-stained valleys, soot-blue peaks,
Milk-gushing springs in marble-curdled alleys,
Diamond-smoking, choking with refused reflections
Of sunset like the slag eruption of a cold volcano:
In all this vividness-to-animality,
A hell for exquisites.
Even with the forecast of the night,

When the horizon is harsh horn of shadow
Scarcely seen,
This gentle bedlam, in its vastness,
Seems serene;
And Death here in black innocence.

IMPERVIOUS FRIENDS

THE MONGOOSE

The fluid mongoose
Is a lively shadow,
More self-contained than the cage.
How many iron bars needed
To circumvent a shape like hidden moonlight?
How many eons of stalking,
Of suffering,
To make the plaintive accent,
Almost half a thought,
That is the wistful horror of his pupil?
He looks at me.
He has already forgotten.
Only the creeping rhythm of his tail,
Gliding,
Back and forth,
Back and forth,
Weaves the subtle design
Of restlessness.

WHITE PEACOCKS

Pompes funèbres,
Should be written over the gateway
Of the fowl enclosure.
Over the roosts, flame the crests,
The white torches.
Hecate stands in the shadow.
If an evil goddess could spin lace for the dead,
Of that would be these flamboyant tails.

A peacock flutters.
It struts.
The demi-oriflamme clouds all the barnyard
With mystery.
Six white peacocks ride at midnight on the shoulders of the hearse.

The peacock's scrawny throat is as withered as leprosy.
The peacock's little eye,
In the painted, feathered head of a bald Pierrot,
Flashes a mindless arrogance.
The fold of its beak is meagre,
Like the mouth of a woman who has grudged the world all,
And grudges,
Even now,
The violence of her disappointment—
Her only passion.

The peacock's little feet
Disdain earth timidly,
But from the stooping, rounded back,
From the defiant, last good-grooming of the plumage,
Springs the ornament of renunciation,
The blenched, regal, final garment:
As if the trees of Paradise had shed,
One by one,
Their still, immaculate fronds,
Covering,
As with an offering,
The starved body that plucks at grain;
And the palm trees of Paradise
Had laid shadows of silver,
And forever,
Upon the trailing avalanche.

If you will be silent, my peacock,
You and your hen who is a lesser likeness,
We may know death beautiful.

CAT

Cat,
Petulantly,
Like a sleek volcano,
Tosses that stiff morsel of inertia—
Mouse.
Cat,
Choking with an arrogance magnificent,
Is dowagerlike.

The demure mouse,
Modestly stunned,
Beyond display of suffering
Yet must rouse
To meet his obligations,
Scramble to escape.

Alas!
In the cradle of torture,
The little weepless one
May lie asleep once more.
Cat,
Like a foretold doom-at-midnight,
Delights,
Innocently.
Mouse,
Not caring to be shriven,
Dies.

HAWK AFIELD

Quail are still.
Coveys are still.
Sparrows might be underground.

Young partridges have ceased to run;
Because of that violence,
Minute upon a peak of air,
Flashing, black-bladed,
Like an evil knife.
Unaided, flickering,
Isolated,
Burns,
Against the flexing turmoil after rain,
The black flame on the vast altar
Garnished for the sacrifice!
Dead grass, herbage, hedge, water,
A pond tweaked by the breeze and afterglow,
Reflect . . . *Him!*
He sears the spirit of a peaceful countryside.
His is the attention of a universe.

He falls.
Heaven plunges with him.
The fixed meadows all collapse.
It is over for the other . . .
Not for the hawk.
Fierce, obdurate, and only half defeated,
Once more aflitter and bereft of victim,
In motion no more than a twinge,
He stands alone to hold the sky.

SINGES MAQUIS

They are called
Coquentin and Mistinguette.
They remember one another languidly.
She tries a peanut with her teeth.
He is less curious yet.
He draws himself

On all-fours
To the dollhouse
Where their marriage bed is laid.
His bannered tail juts insolence
From their small door.
Mistinguette will not follow.
Coquentin returns.
Proximity
Supplies their dreamy days
With tepid continence.

Mistinguette twists involuntary toes
Through the bars of her cage.
One of her mild, insensate paws
Feels buttons on my coat.
Her eyes sorrowfully refuse to speculate.
They are as ruddy as carbuncles.
In these minute circles
Of rage not her own,
Float dots that wonder—
Not too deeply.
Her pig throat grunts,
Affliction half mechanical.
Her little snout trembles.
Coquentin is beside her.
Blindly,
Their separate glances roving,
Upon the florid constellations
Of the people's faces going by,
The pair embrace.
It is good,
This warming that is habit.
Night comes.
The zoo is deserted by the sightseers.
The lion roars,
And shakes,
Somewhat,

The calm
Of their convenient arrangment.

He,
Gazing above,
Makes his defiance to the cat-eyed stars.
She,
With his body for her pillow,
Endures.
They are happy,
Happy,
In their perfect married life!

ON THE INSOUCIANCE OF GULLS

Queen Mary, in the very teeth of war, lays corner stones for hos-
pitals, examines model kitchens for the soldiers, selects, from the lav-
ish offerings of drapers, material for knickers for the Girl Guides.

A gull, nonchalant,
Settles nimbly on a glassy mountain,
Takes a wave as though it were a blossom,
To be broached for honey
By himself, and bees.
A gull, teetering on the frosted hoop of the tide,
Is a ballet master,
Folding away his wings traditionally,
As if he were the Angel Gabriel
On church windows.
He stalks fish.
In the rain-rutted crystal beneath him,
His image,
Caressing devastation subtly,
Is a dim, slow flame.
He clings crabbedly in limpid flight
Upon the soggy air.

In the end,
When promenaders leave the beach,
One gull
Quitting the land-searching swell,
Will hang,
Unmoved,
A floating signal
In his empty watchtower,
While his crossed gaze
That has assumed a bird-bath in immensity,
Turns shrewd with fear.
Can he really *see*
Beyond the mud-green water,
The brown and tarnished rainbow of the twilight?
Is it only to the pitting drizzle that he gives his cry,
So wild and white
Above the whitening spume?
Or is he still sustained
By his robust myopia . . .
. . . like you . . .
Good Royalty?

THE EAGLE

Noble old actor,
Half become the part,
The massive eagle,
Huddled in his loose, dramatic cloak of rusty plumage,
Grips his lean perch.
His gilt eyes are vivid as agony,
Yet they refuse him sight.
He is a prey to the uncertainties
Of mere public opinion.
He stirs.

Night rustles sombre leaves.
His dignity is naked
Under tufts of flung-back feathers
On his brow.

What is the crowd to him?
A despised reason for the calm and mighty flight
Above those lost and dwindling tents of snow.

OSTRICH

If he carried Aladdin's lamps
Beneath the fern-hung hollows of his elbows
It would not surprise me.
On the gnarled stems of his legs
Rises the tower of his dingy splendor.
Lengthy and deliberate,
Like a camel,
He squats in the dust,
His body naked,
Like an old man's skull,
He has planted secretly,
Against the earth,
Hoofs that would not disgrace an elephant.
On goose-fleshed elastic
He unfurls his throat.
The doll-gaze of his eyes,
Beneath his lashes of an actress,
Is unemotional.
He ignores the miracle
That is himself,
And prefers clover,
Plucked stem by stem,
And gulped jealously
From the heap at his convenience.

Is the lily pure?
Behold pink calyxes of ears
And say it is not!
Look at the sow's magnificent compendium:
Teats, thighs, ruddy belly,
And say it is not!
Are digestive organs,
Simon-clean,
Less offensive to the refined spirit
Than the indulgence of more complicated lusts?
Look at the sow's one mind to grub!
Why the adulterer's a fragile, inconclusive creature
In his sinning.
Contradicting all the priests of all religions,
The missionaries to all heathen,
And mothers who provide indulgence
Of a gustatory nature
To their children, after Sunday School,
It is worse, I say, for the soul
To be obsessed and possessed
By desires which focus all their yearning
Along the tongue, esophagus, and whole digestive tract
Than in the nervous centers more connected with imagination!
As Jesus voluntarily did yield himself
That paltry man be saved,
The sow has unwittingly become a victim and a lesson.
Sensible, sensitive people
Will speak politely at a marriage or a funeral,
They will cover up a dying horse,
Yet drag a sow, upon a cruel halter,
Along a public street!
Merely because she is fat-stuffed like a sofa cushion,
Quilted, padded in pink satin,
They ignore it that she is living;
That, living, she was born naked to the world;

Where, due to some negligence I cannot understand,
She has remained naked.

To be crucified,
Or buried in your flesh,
That others may pretend the universe is kindly—
It's the same thing!

THE OWL

Oh, those eyes, those eyes . . .
There is a lamp that burns inward only.
Owl, you are a virgin.
Even though you have a nest in the elm tree,
And four little ones,
Who gape with naked mouths in the darkness,
Asking a bloody feast.

I saw a baby gazing at me,
Appropriating me to its own blank understanding,
And I thought it was whole.
I saw a madman,
As his sly regard used the whole world
For his design.
I saw a woman in a church
Looking through death
To find her need-created god.
When I was instructed by these people,
I had not beheld you, Owl—
Not rightly.

I had not taken account of your solemnity,
While you sit,
Still under your umbrella of speckled feathers,
As a man will sit when he is caught in a rainstorm.

I had not interested myself in the Roman dignity
Of your profile,
Your beak pressed to your throat
In immovable orthodoxy.
What an attitude!

Yet, lest I jibe,
And think your self-assurance merely complacent,
You shift one of those silk screens that are your eye-lids,
Sheltering mystery;
And the well of night,
In the center of the glassy furnace,
Displays the velvet flame of the Demon,
In the spell that makes you Diana's.
Then, as very defiance of the day,
Fallen upon you like a blow, stupidly,
You cry—
Utter a grey sound made at a dawn in Limbo.

I shall suspect, hereafter,
That you are a poet:
Neither your friends, nor the sufferings of your family,
Nor your victims,
Important to you.

THE GOAT AND THE GAZELLE

The goat from the Atlas Mountains
Does not fear me,
Even though his hoofs
Are as tortured to uselessness
As a mandarin's finger nails.
There are still his horns;
Spirals of granite,
Eroded by all the centuries of wind

Blown up the crags
From which his ancestors have looked
On forgotten races of men.

The gazelle
Is more the lady.
From liquid eyes
That are prominent as with disease,
She questions what I have to offer.
The very crescent moon above her brow
Accents her panic.
Her meager ankles are as stockinged reeds.
Her feet, discreet apostrophes to haste.
Yet she controls herself.
Her face presses the bars of her enclosure.
Her tight nostrils, that swell with curiosity,
Insist, implacably.
If I retreat, she approaches.
If I advance,
She calculates the fitting instant for escape,
In gestures I have met before.
The goat,
In his hoary blanketing of youth,
Believes himself splendid.
But that gazelle . . .
She loves me;
Allows me to disturb her,
To set her brush of tail to twitching,
Her white belly to heaving with anxiety,
While she scatters her small, cautious droppings
So abandonedly!

The litter of squirrels
Would arouse the compassion of the Virgin Mary.
The hyenas,
With shuffling slope of back,
With foreheads lunging,
In over-cerebral development,
Lombrosianly,
As their stale eyes,
Dusty and prominent,
Meet your own,
Are really beyond the values of cruelty.
An old monkey,
With her baby,
Displays,
On the moth-eaten fur of her breast,
The glossy circles of teats wrung slack.
Her pink face,
Nude in its shock of yellow hair,
Elongates.
With a snout of derision,
She fulfils her obligations,
Baring her yellowed canines:
Then returns to her carrot,
Quarrelling for it with her infant.
The panther,
A baby in gloves,
Springs,
Loose-hipped,
On sponge-soft paws,
To one end of her closet of confinement,
And returns.
Her jellied eyeballs clear with her secret,
Her blank pupils deride the ghosts
That are spectators.
Too calm for illusion,

She scrubs,
With her meaty feet,
The stiff glass whiskers
That prick her jaws.
In her chaste orgy,
Lumberingly voluptuous,
She abandons her length
To our observation;
Rolls, wallows,
Tries vainly to exhaust herself.
When the man with the basket of mutton
Can be smelled,
Distantly,
Ardor,
Like a glacial fire,
Wells in a gaze
Bold enough to place cats
Over all in Egypt.
Her snarl rends her joyously.
Her weighty tail shudders.

But the little painted duck is diving in the pond,
And the dapper bantam cock
Conducts himself with all the resolution of a general,
Though more tastefully.
The dun snake,
Flat under the fine wire grating,
Is a coil of poisonous dust,
Its fat head sleeping,
A firm lozenge on the ground it loves;
Its distrustful spirit closed
In the torpor men have fed it.

Oh, God, would God I were a Presbyterian,
And could feel these creatures
Less real than I!

OTHER PEOPLE

CHOPIN'S GRAVE REVISITED

Little boys are tramping home from school.
Little girls are tripping home from school,
With nursery governesses.
It is raining.
The trees lurch and huddle in a silver torment
Up and down the street.
In the suburban parlor,
Behind clean curtains, polished windows and pots of aspidistras,
Katie, in a frock also clean and new,
Practices her mazurka.
Lofty with its *beauté du diable*,
The mazurka stamps on its lamb's feet,
Keeps the pace of Katie's metronome.
The poplars in the garden wail louder than Chopin's chords.
Katie's pig-tails swing,
As she persists to time,
And sturdily regards the rhythm and the rhyme.
Katie's playing in the firelight is food for a lean belly.
An odor of nursery teas and damp linen burdens the air.
How innocent the clouds that lie
Like sooty bruises on the foggy London sky,
On short November afternoons.

FOR EMILY BRONTË

This beating on the door
Began in the first hour:
Iron fist beating
A little lamb's greeting:

Rap of brazen knuckles pounding,
Heart and helpless being sounding
To the dry
Beat, beat, beat.
And no way out . . .
Not any way,
Until the last day.
Oh, helpless spirit of me
That would live in sun
And had a mind to sing,
Why were you chosen for the habitation
Of this arid, unseen thing?
What, with this brutal urging,
When death has made an open way and wide,
Will come crashing through?
This raging guest in a guileless breast,
My lamb, it isn't you!

FOR A CELEBRATED FRIEND

Colder, colder . . .
Is the grip tightening about his heart
The hand of the buried?
Is the sense of his mind emptied by the panic of the hurried
Disaster that has come upon him?
Have the warm and living hours betrayed him?
This is fame!

The moments of the beautiful are lonely.
Flowers never bloomed upon a trampled street.
The echoes from the hinterlands of lovely thought
Are never audible
Where worldlings meet.
Voices out of the strange vastness that he used to hear
Have ceased their crying.

The mind we once would praise or blame with clean severity
Is dying.
A phantom marionette strides on the sky.
He asks: Is it I?

THE ACE

Over the little plot of graves
Precious with ornaments of suffering,
With white crosses,
The grass green cool as snow,
And great elms bared,
Like frozen, prehistoric feathers
Waving on the afterglow,
In the pink chiffon sunset,
The air plane passed,
Snoring,
Ravaging the still air.
People were walking softly,
Filling the empty vases
With the beggary of autumn gardens.
Riding on the yellow splay,
Like glistered fingers,
That were gripping all the west,
The stiff-winged aeroplane went by,
Ploughing blackening quiet
Through the pulseless, ruddy sky.
People stopped, and wonder grew,
As with the fall of dew.

SUCCESSFUL MEN

I often wonder at the gallantry of fools,
The fearless, paltry things they do,
Insipid wisdom in the ready lie.
They tilt with never-vanquished gods.
They live as those who cannot die.
The archangels are formed in steel.
They have no souls, to bleat and strut.
Life, in her parading of religions,
Is a pious slut.

A HISTORY

I

She stripped off her fine dress.
Her flesh beneath I found
Was fairer far,
And sweet.
But it needed the hothouse heat.

II

I went to a land
Where there was sun
To warm our bed for nakedness.
I had to take a gun.

III

I fled from all that freshest feels
And looks.

I tried to see the sun,
And scent the earth,
In books.
I reached the monastery gate,
And peace—I hoped.
I had not come too late.
Withered I was, with sunken loin.
The monks they welcomed me—
When I had dropped a coin.

IV

I was bellyshackled still
With dread.
I stayed so
While I groaned for bread.
I am free, at last—
In the house of the dead.

WALLS FOR SLEEP

They have not done much for the world,
But they are little brothers in Christ.
Their beds are narrow
And the spreads of grass have begun to wither.
They are little brothers in Christ.
The wax flowers are not very handsome
After all these years.
The glass bells are broken.
But the little brothers and their sisters
Are asleep in Christ.
Some were nearly a hundred years of age
When they were laid here.
The youngest was an infant.

There were others not sixteen.
Sleep is long and life is only for a little while.
They are asleep in Christ.

Over the cemetery wall,
Just a little way over,
A man steers a plough.
The gulls flow after in a hungry harvest,
To squat beside the billows he upturns.
The gulls scream, mew;
Rise and dazzle the air.
The little brothers and sisters in Christ
Stir faintly under the clouding loam,
Lest they find sleep longer, longer—
And the cemetery walls
Not high enough.

TO A ROMANTIC LADY

Her fresh, clean stare
Was like heaven
When rain has washed it of all clouds
And subtleties.
She never knew how wild she stood,
Soulless as a mermaid in her lair,
With her unbound hair;
Too young, too lovely to endure
The wound that always bled,
That left her like the dead.
She was on the edge of a sea.
It flowed immeasurably between her and the others:
Parents, husband, children, brothers.
She was on high ground, alone.
She was breathless with disaster.
She was near, too near,

Where nothing is at all.
She dreaded the fall.
She waited,
On the rim of everything;
With her breathless stare,
With her eyes bare
Of all but the last thought:
Should she—should one—ought
She to go on and find . . .
Or had she left the thing she sought
Behind?
She ran,
Returning to the deepest wood,
So strange to her, so isolate . . .
Yet solitude was good,
With sun,
Mercurial upon the dew,
And a last patch of blue
Above kind trees.
(Or is that kind without a mind?)
She was not a stone
To die alone!
She was young. She was rosy, yet,
And white.
She listened to the feet of the world.
She would not leave the acre she had half possessed,
Where the dream was hers . . .
And good.
There she stood.
Forever?

NIKE

(On reading the early poems of H.D.)

You, on a sea-rock, swift through the dawn
In the emptiness of morning:
Harsher, more beautiful than light
Which blinded your stone eyes,
Your face, upraised.
Was it joy that killed you,
Or was the small, cold ivory flower
You held against your breast
Too white?

WRITTEN IN A DISCOURAGING EPOCH

(To C. K. S.)

The warmest accident of harmony
Is his whole being,
Greater than can be envisaged
By design;
Yet, in this life,
He moves half-recognized
Because he has no kind.
Men cannot weep for gods or heroes.
Men weep for pigmies that are men.
They did not tear their hair
To crucify a Nazarene.
They did not strike their breasts
To see a genius burned.
They will be calm,
They will be satisfied, again.
Lord, if in humility I dare to curse you,
Omnipotent above what's called a plan,

It will not be for lives of sinners,
Or their wickedness,
But for your waste of one good man.

APHRODITE IN WINTER

Beauty,
For a woman,
Is a mirror:
There the goddess crowned
To whom men bend,
At whom the veriest strangers
Stare.
It is—almost—
The mission of a priestess
To braid the broken sunlight
In youth's flashing hair.
The goddess in the looking-glass
Is very generous, is very kind.
She bends to lift up peers
To share with her such utter loveliness
Of heart, and lavish flesh, and unembittered mind.
At forty—or a little more,
The goddess has to change her name,
And fling a stoic's cloak
About her slave-bred nakedness,
Or die of shame.

FOOL

Clever men,
Gay as wasps,
Buzz at suffering,

Sting beauty's ripe fruits,
And avoid being ridiculous
—until they die.

PURITAN'S DAUGHTER

(To Margaret)

Her clean heart
Is like a white stone
Garnished by the sun and wind.
Sometime,
Somewhere,
Another carved upon it
One word: *Sin.*
Since, pondering
The rune she does not understand,
She's not so happy as she used to be.

A PORTRAIT

"The sins of the fathers shall be visited upon the children
Unto the third and fourth generation,"
Said the old lady.
She was grave, of course,
Watching me with her brown eyes,
Her head cocked like a wren,
Settling her spectacles a little higher
On her small, veined nose,
And giving me that stare from nowhere
Which will pass for awful sternness if one does not think.

O Lamb of God, I thought,
She taketh away the sins of the world,
For verily she hath no sins.
How can she speak of hell who has never seen hell?
Nor has she seen heaven, either,
O Lamb of God.

My old lady has seen the way the cloth should be laid on Sunday,
Has seen the quantities of sugar that the vicar takes:
But surely she has not seen hell!
How then, Lamb of the Almighty,
Can she prophesy?
For a prophet is a man—or woman—
Who is nailed to a cross.
A prophet is a man—or a woman—
Who has been tempted by the brighter vision
Of a world outspread,
And has rejected it.
This old lady—
Why she has never burned her fingers under the tea cosy!
O Lamb of God, if I may say so, Lamb of God,
She's much too innocent ever to be a saint.

A NEWSPAPER BALLAD

(In memory of the VESTRIS *November 12th, 1928.)*

Mrs. Dennis, out of cabin forty-seven,
Goes out on deck and stares.
She can hardly make out the sea.
She looks at people reading there in eight,
At Mrs. Grey, combing her hair,
In cabin thirty-three.
The air smells salt, sweet, clean, pure.
It is happy air.

Little flaps, little slaps, little dabs of water
Flaunt at the ship's side.
The sounds are like the sounds on land
With an incoming tide.
This modest fragrance of a salt-dipped rose
Allays her fear.
It's calm. The engines do not pulse.
Yet the lifting shadow of the deepest water . . .
Well . . . it seems a little near.

The corridors, red-carpeted,
They look so safe and fine;
But the stewards watch,
And the sea creeps in,
With its thin, dark, licking line.
O, stewards in the galley,
You huddle grey as lice.
The rumor's out. It's got about.
The prospect ain't so nice.
A port-hole tilting suddenly
Spills stars upon the floor
Where lamps have crashed
And the wet night's in
Through the sill of a broken door.

The dawn flows by like a stream of milk.
It makes the passages all foggy-white and drear.
Some hearts leap up to fall again
As people see their plight too clear.
The captain has ordered an S.O.S.
It's time for folk to hear.

The first life-boats are floundering,
The women in the wreck.
The Old Man sticks in his overcoat
And won't come off the deck.
The captain feels himself alone

Midst brains too froze to wonder,
Or quiver to the bite of foam,
Or hear the ocean's thunder.
Sea-greyed mouths, sea-greyed eyes
Are stunned by staring at too vast skies.
Not many meditate upon their homes today.
Homes seem too far away.

His dread is heavier than waves.
In dread, man fails and clings.
But there's fear so bright
When it comes at night
It gives you silver wings.

"Now, Captain, have a life-belt, man!
Why stay here? Save your skin!"
The captain looks and speaks no word.
The wireless chap jumps in.
Oh, Captain, put your life-belt on!
Oh, Captain, don't come down!
It will not save your passengers
For you to sink and drown.
The sharks are very frequent here.
They find the eating good.
Their fins are steel.
Their eyes are stale.
Their souls are made of wood.

The sea puts up its midnight tents,
With ceilings gold and blue.
The gaping fish are not surprised
When moon and stars slip through.

"Say, fellow, are you black or white?
The deeps are turning red."
"I'm neither black nor white, Captain.
The same as you . . . I'M DEAD."

MATERNITY CLINIC

(To a certain nurse)

Oh, nurse,
Thou acid virgin,
Who hurlest thy despising imprecations,
Scientifically,
On nature's brood,
The large-bellied Italian woman
Has accepted you
Among the other pests.
You cannot be mute
Like the Italian woman.
You have not left to her
Enough of our civilization
To be a covering
For her swollen form.
Yet she does not speak.
Is it necessary, nurse,
Lean one, naked of religions?
Are you selling,
To these pregnant hummocks,
Each squat in apathy,
Awaiting her turn,
Tickets to a fair
At which you preside?
Then you are playing to a gallery
That is undeceived.
Not the loose-mouthed black accepter
Believes in the ritual.
Not the whore once fruitful
Any more believes.
These negligent absurdities,
These mothers,
Though, out of the laboring slime,
They give birth to no more than the high-school education

Of such as you,
Are learned, at least,
In sorrow.
Woman, truculently chattering in jaunty jargon,
The starched apron of your shame is not begrudged.
These gaze upon you humbly,
Surprised at the cleverness with which you make
The clink of tawdry baubles which they recognize
Appear to sound so much.

TO LOLA RIDGE

Blue moths that circle the moon,
The soft stern eyes,
Reflecting bright pain
As sweet lakes reflect the brass of battle.
In them, Mars sees himself,
While mildest virgins bathe secure.
She, whose courage always flings a thousand banners,
Is of all gaudy vanities withholding, and demure.
Her hands are burned transparent,
Like clear alabaster,
By her long shielding of a solitary flame.
A brutal vegetation barred her way.
It gored the air.
It tore her thighs and breast,
And feet so light
Their very running was our rest
When Darkness wrote her fame.
The bitter brambles drew her blood.
The blazing thickets made her smart.
Not one arrow flung upon her
By the blinded
Pierced her shining heart.

I am tired of love songs.
Lilith, Sister of the Serpent's Breath,
Give lovers death.
I am tired of the various forms
That are my seeming,
In their hot dreaming.
The youth I have is not for long.
I will not yield it to their song.

Aphrodite, drag man seaward in your veil,
Make his shroud of all the glittering millenniums.
I would give him a thorn that would pierce his sleep
Where pain is deep.
If he touch me,
Let him find me cold.
Let me wither to a grimace at his gaze.
Let me be old.
I offer my embrace.
He will not see my face.

I must sear his heart with my own burning,
Or, while I lie,
Prone to his eagerness like leaden earth upon my longing,
I will die.
Let misery, sickness, rotting age
Possess him,
As darkness creeps upon those growing blind.
Kill his pride!
Let him lose all that he may find all.
Mary, make him kind.

Like an ant,
Carrying away the particles
Once living things,
The mind carries away
What lived before it,
Placing all here
In the dead heap,
In the mummy case.
Which of you, O Cheops,
When kissed upon the forehead
By the Darker Angel,
Murmured
To feel,
In chilly circles left,
Invisibility?
Which grudges these husks of his sorrows?

To the eyelids of the Colossus,
To the stale mouth of the princess in her cerements
The smile returns.

TO DEATH

AFTERWARD

Love is so unkind, so terrible,
So smoldering and black.
It dries my tears.
It sears and sucks my mind of grief.
It guts me of my every thought.
It makes my charred heart crack.
There is no urge to destruction.
There is no more flame and red.
Jesus, pity white and childish flowers
That spring up timidly out of this wilderness
Where I am dead!

TO O.M.

Put up your eyelids
That are curtains over brown silk tents,
Or close those veils of stone
Against memories.

My arm was a cradle under your pillow.
So is the arm of Death.
My breath was gentle over you.
So, on a breeze also,
Comes the perfume of the rotten flowers
In the vases of the cemetery.

As a child conceals itself,
You turned your face to the darkness.
We were there,
Death and I.

The hairs of your head are springing fine
With the blades of the new grass.
New dust and old dust
Run together.
Sweet, up the hillside,
Are millions of grass blades;
My voice and your voice
Whisper together across the mounds:
Death!
Death!
Indifferently.

THE SACRED GROVE

Deep in the clean rock,
Hemlocks of the forest,
Gaudy with darkness,
Tissuous with wasted sunlight . . .
There are crossed swords between me and the hemlocks.
All the ledges of the waterfall have beards of glass.
Far inward, in the uncolored crystal,
Light is cooling.
Lost spots of daylight lie there,
To be found next year . . .
But not by me,
Because of the crossed swords and the flame.
Even the hill, sugar-yellow with its birches,
Is barred to my way.
Twilight brims,
As if grey tears welled up.
Nobody tries any longer to find roads.
Let the wood rise once again about me
With forgotten auguries.

AUTUMN

The drenched windows of dwellings,
So wild and dim,
Reflect the inward flames.
The corn bends there
In its golden rows
In the pastures of twilight.
Along the street
The auburn trees
Defy the drizzle,
With cold, enigmatic sound,
Until the hesitating evening comes
In mouse-color.
Suddenly, my rage of happiness awakened
Defies even gentle, obscure heaven.
The shower, sly as sly thoughts,
Teasing the crouching roof above my bed,
Gladness-to-be-alive
Springs up with gusto emptying me of words.
I see that a unique treasure is committed to me
—By god-knows-Whom!

NOW AND THEN

Honey flows in the street.
The wind is too lavish.
I could weep with its sweetness.
People met have darling faces at a play.
I find myself at the end of day,
And think;
God has commended me!

ON MY BIRTHDAY

If no one watches with me
These exquisite skies,
If no one,
Looking clearly in my open heart
Sees warm and wounded beauty with my eyes,
If I must live with ecstasy
And live alone,
May I house my guest in stone!

FROM MY WINDOW

City contours are enfeebled by the dusk.
The lamps, new lit,
Flash rosied mirrors on the dark,
On the river, the evening of many waters.
Those clouds,
Already half forgetful of the day,
They are gold with laughter.
The wistful eye of heaven
Is my own.
It is love that lingers.
It is love
Illumining those shoals
Where night is fugitive.
The world, I think,
Is proud with love;
Else why are all the noises of the street
So small?
Clean, like a piece of new-washed silver,
My heart, immersed in this baptism
From I know not where,
Begins to warm my breast again.

Dawn comes like a rainbow in ice.
The trees, in dewy relic of midnight,
Are still and terrible.
Crows sound their derisive trumpets
In caws like laughter
Over wet roads,
Abandoned as to allegory.
The mystery-enveloped light
Seeps fire, with tears,
Into a smoking lake of fog,
Through meadows in crystal and beaten silver.
For the stunned world
In its moist blanketing,
Dappled with green and jet,
The rapt moment to awaken
Is not yet.
Sunless, the fields glow deep
In timid eastern yellow of small flowers.
And I, aroused to hear the silence thunder,
To see wild clouds
In blue the color of pure wonder,
Am borne from dreams
As on the river of my secret smiles.

JOY

My joy ran,
Like a white cry,
Naked through the morning.
In the brightness of rapture,
All the stars were quenched.

Death, I thank you.
Ironically,
But none the less,
I owe my world to your black dress,
Your skull-face and sickle.
You have given me the wisdom of delight
You have made it fiery gallantry to sing.
Joy is the fiercer for the dolor you bring.
I am grateful for an august foe.
Mankind that has nowhere to go,
The people dwelling in our street
Who only live to work and eat:
For all these you have struck the halo.
Your frigid breath has blown the fire
Making desire immeasurable.
Shall I not reverence myself
Who struggles with a god?
And though, at last,
I lie outcast,
Through you I will be ennobled.

LOST

I am of the lost.
I know no shepherd.
I know no fold.
On the mountain
I feel the cold.
Here is no stream
To slake a thirst
As old as mine.
The herd has travelled
To its own security.

It hugs warm stalls
And mangers full
For its maturity.
From heav'n flashes no answer
To the long question
Of the living that is prayer.
Stars . . .
Are the grudging eyes of winter,
Flaming there . . . and there!

THE DROWNED MOTHER

Maybe the hurrying feet I heard,
As I sprang,
Were those of a child.
Maybe the little sounds following—
Maybe those were the footsteps of a child.
Did he run?
Has he tried to reach me?
I should have turned,
Even as I leapt,
Glanced over my shoulder,
And given him the signal to follow?
Would he have thought better of it afterward
Had he crossed the long foam,
The white, wicked fields?
I might have called to him
And told him the truth.
I might have said:
Child, this is peace.
This is the long whisper under currents,
The roar in the shell.
When the wind races clean away from you
And vanishes on the bright sky,
It tells you no more.

Here the black tides of night,
With their breath of alabaster,
Pursue us no more.
We are at rest.
Give your little heart to me,
In my cold hand.
It will never be in safer keeping.
Under the grey-fleshed moon,
The forests of the seaweed are floating
Quietly.
Waves crawl gently in their wreaths of mourning.
My tears have added only a little more salt
To those already shed.
Creep to the beach in the early morning.
Find some trace of me you will remember—
Hat—shoes—a stocking.
Steep yourself in this which has succeeded the other.
Lave your youth.
Grow strong, merry, confident.
Run away again.
Forget.
Always,
Here,
Safe in my coral fingers that are bone and iron,
Your little heart will beat securely,
Pulsing like a little sea thing,
That must warm the two of us.

NIGHTMARE

Fear turns slowly on its hidden pivot.
Hydra heads,
Gaudily ornamented with pain,
Stare . . .
At me who am dread,

And cannot warm a bed.
Pursuit is by the wind,
The sterile wind.
Every decision made
Is a decision to be lonely.
Night is shallow
With its skim of quickening moon.
I cannot abandon memory.
Now that I am old,
It is all I can hold.
I will not be whipped to my grave.
I must have peace.
I feel it near.
I will close my eyes
When the scrawny daylight
On the window blind
Is a pallid sneer.

DELIRIUM

The fever tree is ever green,
Where flaming birds of menace
Roost and preen.
How soft the jewelled pinion
And how wild the throat––
As each pipes indecipherably
The wanton note!
The tree is guarded by the Beast
Who smiles on us,
His cringing feast.
Midst livid roots
The slothful worms
Fatly dispute
Life's fallen fruit.

BURIAL

The leaves hang still.
No insects' shrill
Disturbs the night.
The great moon flings
Out silver wings,
Dripping with light.
Their radiance laves
Forgotten graves.

ELEVATION

Life is a thief of all those treasures of rich longing
My childhood held inviolate and whole,
A cold marauder, carrying away,
Bit by bit, drop by each drop of anguished blood,
Day by every futile striving of a day,
The store of sense that fed a heart and soul.
(Or is there something left
So strangely deep
We only see the shining thing again
When we can lie secure in sleep?)
Pressed by the feckless crowds in unfamiliar cities,
By Thames or Rhone or Danube or the Seine,
Before an arid sunset in Morocco,
In Paris, in a twilight after rain,
I have turned to stare at light,
When pale fire beat with trembling wings
Against a housetop or a mountain,
Ere it withdrew in night,
And thought,
As if my childhood suddenly alive
Confronted me,
As if my angel breathed
On beauty all at once too keen to bear,

Oh, God, I am not dead!
The thing I seek—
The place I seek—
The time I seek,
As though it were appointed,
Has come!
Is—*there*!

WORDS

A line out of a book
May greet you
For the first time
With more familiarity than any face.
Words can be more living
Than the creatures and the furnitures
Of any place.
Someone, never beheld by you,
Forgetful that there is a creed in time,
Writes, upon the margin of another universe,
A stroke in rhyme.
The sign of blood is rosier here
Than ever it has run in human heart and veins.
The flesh that has ignored the very name of flesh
Feels most its pains.
Closer, for an instant,
Are we to one another,
Myself and him of whom I hold no other proof,
Than man and woman,
Breast to breast, primevally,
Without a roof.
Mostly, what is meant to bridge our isolation,
Stands to divide.
When I read the words conceived in solitude,
I know the other at my side.

ONE NIGHT

Above the steely avalanche of roofs
I stared,
At the moon,
Pale with her chilly centuries,
With her single gristly eye.
It was then
I realized myself inviolate,
Since I had to die.
Not my own hand can arrest determination,
Nor my own thought hold me,
Nor my effort save
This suffering to respond to any other suffering,
Or any glittering memory
Flung from the present aspiration
Pierce the future grave.
At last even the gestures of the dwindled will
Renounce the mere appearance that is striving.
Then the heart is still.

WATCHTOWER

When all the ships have gone out
And are the white leaves of the harvest of disaster
On the last fine fringes of the ocean,
And earth is a verge over ruin,
And even stars can be remembered,
Since they are few,
Keep watch, my mind,
So undefiant and alone.

I am dwindled to the meanness of hope.
I cry out with the language of hope,
The voice of tears . . . arousing mockery.
I am rootless with striving.
No one, here about me, knows,
No living creature understands
How harassed spirit,
Pressed upon,
Retreats to seek the beauty-haunted lands.
There silver stags
Take nights by bounds,
And reach harsh mornings
All too soon.
Yet they strike to light
Whole firmaments
On the metal rind of the moon.
World, your net has cords that bind me.
They are strong and coarse and red.
I break them. I am bleeding.
But I am not free . . . or dead.

MENE MENE TEKEL UPHARSIN

At Balthazar's feast,
There was at least one man of wisdom.
In my own city,
Where stars remain,
Even among the advertising signs,
No one lives
Observant of the lucid writing of the planets,
Fierce today as before,
In the myriad youth of their antiquity.

Definition,
That is a cornering of emptiness,
I shed to its core.
Nothing—
All that is left—
Burns but the more.
The Word *is*.
The Word is I.
No destruction will avail me,
With mind that is stripped too naked keen
To find its covering
In a lie.
In this universe
Without a shelter,
My gaze,
Divested of protecting socket,
Turns,
Unwilling,
Back,
To trace the creeping myrmidons of chaos
Along a level track.
Though I rebel,
In naked longing,
I cannot flee
My own loathly inheritance
Of immortality.
I am conclusion for the footless races,
Fruit
Of the stolid passion
Of their blood ascent,
I, who have been weakly warmed to tenderness
Since ice,
That made life sluggish to its brutal being
Went.
The restlessness of all the waters of the ocean

Is only motion.
The painless vegetation springs and dies.
The forests mount.
They fall,
As suns retire,
As shadows sleep,
Out of monotony of million million centuries
Into a timelessness as deep.
I, from such procreative ennuis sprang.
Of the Vast, Cruel and Serene
I am the helpless part.
Yet, in my pity-poisoned breast,
The Word breathes—
Wordless as before.
Oh, God,
This sodden matter
Has a heart!

LO, HE STANDS AT THE DOOR

If I open the door,
I die.
Let me fasten the door against the clawing wind.
What more can be expected of me, Lord,
If I am kind?
My heart twists with the sight of the first leaves.
They are too young and pale and bright
To bear the brutal, flashing light.
Things must not waken.
Beauty is born to be stricken.
He who is the friend of all distress
Must guess
How, with resuscitation of this loveliness,
I suffer.
If I open the door tonight—

If I stare—
Find nothing there?
No wind upon my face, no kiss of space!
Nothing, nothing, nothing!
The vast terror urging,
And—nothing,
As before.
I will fling back the door.
Now!

There is—
What?

TOMORROW

Deep as murder,
Deep as red,
Deeper than thoughts
Of people dead,
Dark the heavy earth
Will lie,
Mountains of blackness
Upon each eye.
My mouth,
That has pressed in ecstasy
The light, the white, the bitter, fragrant rose,
Will smile
On the bitterness and whiteness of the ages
Of glacial, unending
Snows.
My heart,
Made to start and tremble,
Will be still
As a small bird
Sunk to wither rigidly

Upon the icy plains.
It will be lost,
Asleep,
Forgotten,
Deep.

NIRVANA

When a stone falls through eternities of space,
Does it *feel* slow falling?
When blind eyes are steady in a sun-glare,
Have they fire or sight?
When the secret darkness hides, unbroken,
And withdraws itself in morning,
Does it carry with it,
In a dimness ever further, never spoken,
Morning light?

TRIUMPH

The silver splinter is the clean fin
Piercing the empty nostril.
Browsing fish are at home here.
The sponges float fat flowers.
The ripe anemones are clotted blood.
The coral grips me with its livid fingers
In their millions,
And builds me to a tower!

(Dorchester Square, London)

I

In the operating room,
In the webbed glare,
Tall spiders in white aprons.
In the glass boxes
Of their dry aquarium,
Yawn metal teeth.
The fat anaesthetist
Fits on your diving cap.
Then,
Rip-pling-ly,
The years pass.
(A lizard crawls over a boulder.
A cloud melts.)
If you struggle,
Through the rich numbness,
The nurse says: "Don't worry.
It's all right."
Then you turn up meanings
As a mole turns slugs in dirt.
A still shaft of fire
Seeps through a crevice.
One fine, vibrating cry
From another patient
Inaugurates sensation.
The black and white illusion
Vanishes!

II

All through the wards
The pupate lives
Lie still,
Cocooned in cots,
While nurses,
Brows bound in the stiff curtains
Of Egyptians,
Make neuter progress
From cell to cell.
Diseases flame forth in their radiant colors:
Blossoms of cancer,
Syphilitic flowers,
And other posies, fever bright,
Formed carefully.
These are gardens, gardens,
For life to grow in,
Thoughtfully tended.

III

In the morning,
In the highest branch outside the window,
The sun flies like a gilded bird.
Hyacinths shudder on white plaster walls.
Light blenches even the white dresses of the nurses
With a marigold flush.
At evening, after macerating hours,
Miracle!
Passive as ancient loam,
The sick body,
Feeding the blossoms,
Has reared upon our twilit ceiling
One crushed, enormous poppy.

IV

The violets,
In vases at the bedside,
Curve wildly under shields
Of brass-green leaves,
Disclosing purple,
Darker, darker,
As we look.
The Square,
With bare trees,
Wet and quiet on the rain,
Is a screen of mist-blue porcelain.
Twisting, in the mirrored silk,
Spring strangling, multiform embroideries
Of black coral.
In the deep nothing of the window,
The fire glides,
With transparent petals.
Between me, and the enameled landscape,
And something other, yonder,
My own heart, rosy, trembling,
Leaps . . . *afraid.*

V

I draw back the curtains,
And see, with their million fluttering tendrils,
The windy gardens of the chimney pots.
Curdled streamers, quick as battle,
Are shaking all the roofs of London
With rain-thistled mist.
There's a far-off shudder of smoking brush
On the egg-pale sky.
March gardens,

Secret houses:
Out of them . . .
Hurricane!

VI

Little room,
White like a chapel,
I leave you.
You are a comb
Gutted of honey;
Used . . . and for her sake.
So am I less frightened of one
Smaller . . . narrower.
Tonight,
There is straw laid in the street.
In the first warm wind
Will be a poem I cannot explain.
The soft moon hovers . . .
Sits there brightly on the ledge;
And *her* silence
Is *our* silence,
So long awaited . . .

THE GRAVESTONES WEPT

PART I

1

In the grandmother's garden
In the South,
Spring came early,
But the water in the fountain basin
Was like brown autumn
The year round.
There six goldfish stagnated
And delicately burned the shadows
With their dreaming fins.

The garden wall was adamantly high.
The girl was afraid.
She ran six steps toward the locked gate.
She listened for the moon.
It rose up solemn,
Sending down its secret
From another place.

The moon,
Like a shallow mirror,
Hung from a chimney,
While in the strange road
Lost people passed,
Speaking inscrutably
Of future times.

2

In the freshness of morning
Clean sand was awake.
The frivolous, small fiddler crabs
Took charge of dawn.
At that hour,
Every little creature,
Reaching from its tomb,
Demanded its freedom.

In piney corridors along the shore
Were twenty-thousand masts of ships,
Casting leagues of shadow
For their anchorage,
Deep into the dainty silence
Of the sea.

At night,
The girl slept restlessly,
Dreading the visions
That betrayed, to her, reality—
A reality so much her own,
But tenuous,
The manifests as yet too frail . . .

3

In the glass, in her room,
She had surprised her silken belly,
Hollowed hips, and white-stemmed legs.
Before this image
She moved stealthily,
Uneasy with an Unknown sacred to her,
Whom she dared not quite approve.

4

What carved the faces of the poor
Into such bitter effigies?
What knowledge of her ignorance
Impelled them to reject her?
Their brute words of insult
Left her accused of her unlikeness to them,
And this,
With the sin of her grace,
Began to trouble her.

Was it for something false in her father
The poor despised her?
Had her mother offended their need?
Because her grandfather was lavish with trinkets,
Must she deny him, who, of all, was the most kind?
Should an old man be broken
Because of destitution somewhere?
Was life, for her, to be an atonement
For lacks in her elders?

5

Loving her,
Forgiving her dissimilarity,
Her grandfather died.
Coveting her love,
Begrudging her the love of others,
Her grandmother, also, died;
While, for a space,
Haunting her in the eyes of her mother,
Whom her father did not love,
And who loved her daughter
With disappointed passion,
Until death

Removed life's sting,
And the meager thing she had relinquished
Became the larger
That it was renounced.

6

Quiet the young heart!
Make it beat less!
Will the girl be a slave forever?
Is she bound to her nameless hopes?
When dawn rises higher than darkness,
Her elation leaps with it,
In pain of delight!

The moon is heavy on the garden.
Foliage wastes, swamps smolder,
The world is brass.
What is there in her that refuses resignation?
She is tired of her body.
It might as well be given away.
Shall she consign it to mankind?
Or shall the business end with gas, a rope,
Her father's pistol?

Pity her, Moon,
As you shed your light
On forgetful Creation!
Deliver the too-alive!
Teach her for the last time.

She has read the words of Juliet,
Who was fourteen years old.
She is older, but not much,
Yet some day she will be thirty—forty!
Do not abandon her to the years.

No sweet assassin seeks her, Moon!
Send him.
This is the ripe moment.

7

He is no faceless murderer with hairy loins.
He is the boy next door,
Who reconnoiters her over the fence,
And resents her,
Since she wants more than compliments,
And more than he,
With hands and lips,
Can offer her in tribute.

8

In the strong hush of morning,
She awakens to the sun as to a welcome,
And the scales of her blindness
Are the silver of cloud.

She has finished with people,
And trusts only an animal speechlessness
She seems to share.
Still, as she breathes,
She does ecstatic justice to the air,
The attainment of each mid-day is a progress,
She spends herself humbly with the afternoon,
Feeling even gnats and mosquitoes,
Traveling their lives,
Best belong where they are.
And her greed to be of the world,
And to be everything in it,
Declines happily, with successive twilights,

To a final instant before nightfall
When it is a pleasure to be nothing at all.

9

The young hunger.
Youth starves in a coffin she will shatter.
She goes to libraries to read,
And sits in awe and disappointment with Confucius,
And in bafflement and awe with the Buddha.
Plato, Aristotle and Spinoza
Tell her, at length, of a knowledge eventually to be hers.
She is up to Berkeley, Hume,
The eighteenth, then the nineteenth century,
And remains a ghost, contemplating shadows.

She is what youth has been and is to be,
And is not cured! . . .
Did some sickness of the planets
Enter into her at birth?

10

Wherever thought is shaped by living,
She senses life.
So spring has not ceased to tease her with promises,
And she can be wrecked, as ever,
By trees surprised in brilliant bloom.
The moon-filmed nights of summer,
Vast in isolated sculpturing,
Fill every lap save hers,
And can overwhelm her
With mere echoes of her own light tread.

Autumn, to one so tender,
Is a cold hell.
And as winter blesses with oblivion,
Its ravishment of white fields
Becomes too bitter-beautiful to be endured.

11

But there has been a carpenter in Nazarus
As untaught as she is,
And he has not despised women.
And though her reason
Has robbed him of his godhead,
She wishes to resemble him,
And make of her emotions
A mission to mankind.

She would be a Socialist
—a radical of some sort—
And sacrifice herself
For humanity's sake!
And she longs for the holocaust
In which the poison of mortality
Will be consumed.

12

She would have squandered every smallest wonder
Of her young existence,
Her urge to song, the tears she wept,
Her blood—!

This was not enough!
They wanted bread.
She had flung herself into the fire

From which no phoenix arises,
And she is grateful to him who comes
Saying, "I will take your gifts."

13

Now, at last, she is with child,
And with beauty in every part of her,
Her heart, lungs, mind and belly together
Are fashioning the infant she is to bear,
And knowledge has become for her
How to do what she must with perfection.

14

Whom did she affront in his birth?
Were her agonies their revenge?
Who was jealous of her pride and contentment?
Whose tyranny has tortured her child into life?
She would have had him emerge
From her dream into the world,
Smiling . . .

Instead, they are like strangers,
Mutually alarmed,
Able only to mingle their cries of protest
Against an alien surrounding
Hostile to both.
And as his sucking lips
Drink avidly of her being,
She knows she has done him a wrong
For which her milk can be no compensation,
Though gentleness is at its source.

15

She is still young
When the years begin to deal with her stealthily.
And as she weaves for her son
The garment he is to wear among men,
She remembers how soon she, also,
Grew satiate with affection,
And it seems to her she forges
From her very entrails,
The knife ready to his hand,
And for her heart.

Once she was without guile,
But convinced he will desert her,
She is twisted to a purpose
And considers bargaining again
With a father,
Before existence can become as empty
As her womb.

Was it thus
—she asks—
Women first deceived?

16

What gods concede absolution
For the sin of loving too many?
She is replenished,
But parenthood is a divided universe,
And while the male has sowed seeds at random,
She has been building her children a home
Foreordained to dissolution . . .

17

The flesh has lied!
Joy, recollected,
Is like the memory of a crime!
Amidst these lewd and lean of spirit,
Who reverences her truth?
Chant with her raucously, O, winds.
Shout last obscenity!
Deride her though you may,
Time tells implacably
Without a word . . .

18

Little first child,
—wanderer—
Hail!
From the dead love comes wisdom,
And perhaps wisdom will take root here.
Is this grassy hillock
Already a grave in flower? . . .

TO A SNAKE IN EDEN
—1934—

I follow the preying, innocent eyes of you,
Nursemaid of loathing,
As you wind your monstrous wish
In the rim of the nest
And descend the tree unfuriously,
The young bird's heart already beating
In your iron throat.

Glide on to the next disaster,
You born so forgetful,
You have given horror its home.
You are the very bowels of a thought
Brought hideously to life by sun.
You had sunk your deep fang in my sorrow
Long before we met.

So you who are the very shape of unbelief,
Having wounded a summer,
Slip out of Eden!
Purveyor of hospital murders,
Yet comfortable with the grass and silence,
Has faith itself perhaps been nourished
By some memory of the wavering pillar of your body
In its liquid stone? . . .

SCIENTIFIC COMMONPLACE
— 1940 —

A ceaselessly respiring life
Unfolds before the fluoroscope,
As lungs are dwindled, mean with grief,
Or bellows-brightened by the lift of hope;
While in the boney thicket of the diaphragm
The trapped heart struggles
Like some lost and senseless lamb.

Blood paces and slow arteries pound,
Speeding the thought that may outlast its time
And when the labyrinthine nerves are still,
Invisibly continue to proclaim the will,
Although the brain from which thought sprang
Be less than dust,
And cloudy flesh, now dimly seen

In metamorphosis by liver, bladder, spleen,
Has fallen as it must;
And the pelvis, like the skeleton of hands outspread
To bless the head of the unborn,
Has crumbled, and the tree and fruit
Are both long dead . . .

Yet split these vessels
In which joy and tenderness abide,
And wherein sorrow, rapture and ambition hide,
And drain, with cruel, cryptic knife, each vein,
Until mere ligaments are left,
—a skein to fling to chaos!—
If what remain be but a mangled and misshapen thing,
Of this is miracle:
Dark power of living immanent in death!
Death present indeflectibly
In every transient human breath!

OLD AMERICAN STOCK
—1939—

The old man on the apple-barrel
Shut his jackknife and lay down
When they began to build the town.
He cautiously abandoned whittling
When the undertaker said,
"Please hurry! Here's a comfortable bed!"
And he stretched himself at length
To muse, instead, upon some vis-à-vis
Among the stars . . .

Since then, new city lights have blenched the clouds,
And people have all vanished from their shrouds,
Where once rustling corn, half-seen,

Nightly, caught dim reflections from the windows
Of the general store
And the illumined druggist's vials next door;
And now there are other trials
Accompanied by a stench of gasoline,
As filling-station salesmen guide a nation
Along routes designed for regiments in cellophane.

And at the World's Fair, nineteen-thirty-nine,
The neon signs and sputtering electric fountains glow
More brightly than the fronts of pharmacies
Of years ago;
And nixies burble,
From loud-speakers by the lake,
Of late and modish cures for stomach-ache,
Or brawl,
From the veranda of the Hickory Bacon Palace,
In praise of Nibbly Candies,
That, by model manufactury, translate Alice
Into a fresh Wonderland
And a vernacular not at the old man's command.
        —*among cracker-boxes, gingersnaps and farming-tools,*
        his defunct cronies sat and cogitated,
        sighed and spat . . .
Today, an amazed crowd gapes at the Duffield Dairy Cows;
The Red Queen, standing on a soap-box, vows
Hand-milking poisons.
Here patent milkers pump depravity from herds
Subdued by scientific words
Unknown to elk and buffalo . . .
        —*still we detect a smell combined of starch and calico*
        from Mother Hubbards dangling in a row,
        like ghosts of female suicides, escaping Hell
        and returned to deride male counterparts,
        alive and yet despised,
        outcast from modern, liberal arts . . .

Meanwhile, within the Perisphere,
In mystic gloom,
Beneath the rondures of a Moslem's tomb,
The disembodied voice of Mr. H. V. Kaltenborn talks on
In understatement to the music of the spheres
—or rather radio, that gives our folk-ways punch and go—
About the march of youth,
And someone offers time-proof roofing
Not procurable before . . .
—and lanterns fixed in timbered grooves,
shake to a thud of horses' hooves;
a stranger, cynosure of philosophic eyes,
stamps in, slaps snowflakes from his thighs,
and pulls the gum-drop stopper
from the coal-oil tin . . .

around, the furtive drifts shift to and fro,
and winter listens as men think,
tilt up the cider-jug and drink,
and are unmindful of the opera-bouffe
soon to immortalize with truth
the uniting of comrade Stalin
and the advertising boss . . .

For the old man on the apple-barrel
Shut his jackknife and lay down
When they began to build the town,
And had small use for him;
And he was thankful for a bed,
And for the spotless coverlid December spread
Above him . . .
And when spring broke earth's crust,
He was glad of his dust,
As the earth was a thing he understood,
And his coffin, at least, was authentic good wood.
He was simple and plain,
His wants never vain, . . .
—he has no wish to live again—

156

IN YOUTH, OUR HOPE: YOUTH MOVEMENT
—1938—

1

Impervious young,
We watch your midges' dance about time's brink
As you turn on the radio, to chatter and to drink.
At Junior Proms, when you convene in metal-furnished rooms
With those who would assist the preparation
Of the harvests of your tinny wombs,
Your virgin bosoms heave pneumatic sighs,
And even tears, occasionally, slip from your vacant
Lustrously mascarraed eyes.
Ah, Juliet! Ah, Marguerite!
You will not die at sweet sixteen:
Your deaths were terrible and slow,
And happened long ago.
How greener than mere natural reeds and grass
Are rushes made of canvas, paint and wire
By a dramatic class!
Like new Europas,
Rebound to the wheel of speed,
You shriek delightedly with every revolution,
So assured are you, you cannot bleed.
Yet somehow, where all pulse-beats are a brazen drum,
Spring that is grief and glory has refused to come.
It is the loveliest season,
But its compounding of gossamer joy and Delphic woe
Is not for little goddesses of men who run the dynamo.

2

Great Dead,
Tormented, crucified

For steadfast vision,
By the multitude who lie,
Look out on Hades!
Beat those burning, broken wings
Against these walls!
Here are housed fillies in their stalls!
They have read Dostoevski as a credit-count,—
But was he Metro-Goldwyn or a Paramount?
They're Christian misses, though with superstition done
Their sociology annuls all risk of martyrdom.

Great Dead,
Who have foretold the future
In perfected retrospects,
You sow no seed in virgin wombs,
Yet maybe in some dreary pub
An aged drab, communing with her beer,
Broods, on the rim of thought,
Life writ in agonies
As you have writ yourselves:
She drinks her fill,
And suddenly her cup is sweetened,
And you have your audience still.
Wisdom abides in old, scathed arteries.

ALL IS VANITY, SAYETH THE PREACHER
—1943—

South wind is water, and the cup of jade,
As once more little humans wake to sip
The vessel that has snow upon its lip
And over-flows with steel green, knife-cool shade.
Its surging calm like lakes where children wade,
The burnished grain pours on the mountain's hip
A fertile torrent without seam or rip,
From fields man's stressful springtime labors made.

This is illusion's season, those will say
Who fear to taste of Lethe in today!
Drink quickly, then, lest tyrant mind,
Forever aping God, become unkind,
And leave your senses but a bitter brew
Compounded of such summer dawn and dew.

PIKE'S PEAK
—1932—

The shell-frail sky but wanly holds
The large, sad sagging of the mountain's pleats,
Its sumptuous, arid, granite folds.
Below, the trite town squats,
Commemorating the puerility of man,
And silly motor-cars, on silken ribbons of paved streets,
Shoot by between the stucco villas,
Contrived, with aimless tawdriness,
From treasure of degutted stone.

Yet better no despising word be spoken,
As the bare trees, in a quick divinity of nakedness,
Flash in the melting rapture of the west,
And sun, dwelling at last in mist,
Is rosy as a robin's breast,
While majesty that does not sneer
          —so mild sublimity,
             though terrible
             and near! —
Beams kindly on the name of Pike,
Where high, high, high,
Are haunches of the shriveled earth
Refusing birth
To less than greater worlds than ours.

Out of half-hidden ranges, in their chill, residual hue
Of grape-dark mourning, signals dusk,
And lamps in houses are like grave-sweat dew
As the remaining light flies swift from day's abysmal edge
To saturate a single alabaster ledge.

Goodnight to Pike!
There is no evil and no good up there,
No cowardice, no bravery.
Too utter for these late comparatives
Such swollen grandeur of rock chastity!

Come, storm, dragging shadow over ambered glitter
Along roads on which the motors twitter!
Come, vast sorrowless sorrow of the evening,
To salute the life that was before the living
And a cruelty that anteceded crime!
Soon time will fade, too, in that angry blue,
In the bitter silver of the snow.
The land has spoken. We need never speak again.
It has all been said for us and the dead.
This peak is end, and it will take no future imprint
Save from glimmers cast by passing stars . . .

APOCRYPHA
—1939—

To negro poets, living and dead

Sometimes I feel like a motherless child,
Where rue grows fast and hemlock wild
As brambles in a ditch.
Swing low, sweet chariot;
Let me be carried upon song
A long way from home.

Rush on, Great Wings,
While black and white
Dance, golden-shod,
About your flight.
Lead, Moses! Tell all peoples, "Go!"
On love upborne as Jesus' Grace
Flings rainbows over barren space.
Down here is only a dark river murmuring.

Deep river, crossed upon a sigh,
Our drownéd eyes still search for sky.
O, Sister, do not mourn
To find our dank hair floating by.
O, Brother, of such nothingness we are
As is the moonlight and the star.
Roll Jordan! We are as the sand
That silts to make a foreign land.
We are resigned.

Races no longer undefiled
Will never waken to the piercing, mild
Encouragement of Gabriel's horn,
Or see old Jordan rift lethargic mud
And pour, in morning-riven flood,
Toward tides Eternity becalms . . .

We weep. He never said a mumblin' word,
And yet His silence can be heard!
O, let us steal away . . .

1

—1934—

This happened before!
These pines, bewildering the afternoon
With sad, dark cloud;
These leaves, stirring so recollectingly
On relaxed vines,
Were in some former place.
In this moment of terrible plenitude
  —of grass, seed, rich foliage and ripe pod,
    all drunken in forgetful sun—
The generations of indignant are absent,
And the flesh is no longer accused . . .

Oh, well I know how little it counts
Who wrenches fruit from boughs over-loaded!
Yet the hour is one for mortal love—
The least, best thing sprung from summer,
And doomed—*gloriously*!

2

—1938—

The roads are brands on dead flesh,
The brooks lie limp and austere,
Frozen ponds are pools of sugar,
The sleek roofs of farms
Drip crystal above unpeopled houses,
And deer, running the uplands,
Tread with hooves the leaf-mold beds
Soundlessly,
Their wild flight somber,
Like silence itself.

Pure-limbed hill,
Stark to winter rain-tears,
Snow dappling your flanks
Like a melted accretion of antiquity,
You are but bared of deception.
Here child and man can weep together,
Emptied of years' meanings;
Yesterday's grief gathered with tomorrow's,
Kindly, kindly—
As those are kind
Who do not cease to speak of death.

ON BEHALF OF THE INARTICULATE
COMMEMORATING A REJECTED MAGAZINE ARTICLE
DEALING WITH THE NEED FOR BOTH SOCIALIZED
MEDICINE AND PRIVATE MEDICAL PRACTICE

—1940—

Outside the narrow window begins sky
In which devouring and devoured
Can venture speculatively
Only a little way;
Inside is meager, artificial day
Supplied to those who compute joys
In terms of dimes and cents:
The sole adornment on an enigmatic wall,
The picture of the model prison
Completed by the State last fall
On land whereon the heart itself
Is over-trodden ground.

Petitioners before this bar
Are left to concentrate unwillingly
Upon a general doubt of life,

And Miss Rivera
    —with the violet-shadowed
    Spanish eyes—
Lifts her thick, beaded lashes,
Gnaws the lipstick on her trembling mouth,
Undoes her leopard jacket,
And—
    since Justice is a racket—
Resigns herself to worlds in which there can be nothing kind.
While even the hygienic drinking-fountain in a corner
Whispers through the close, submissive air,
Of the despair that comes
When you have done your time.

And the stenographer whose dimples
Struggle through her acne pimples,
Scans disdainfully these bitter meek
Who stand forever at a barricaded door,
And tells the Carib with the scar,
"Don't you know where you are? Sit down!"
And she minces off with a display of bosoms
That were salients in a disappointing year.

And the Carib, hugging to his chest the letter that he cannot read,
Sinks, gingerly, upon a chair
And tugs distraughtly at his stallion's hair,
And stares—
    remembering what furtive deed,
    by hut in thicketing of thatch,
    its gaping threshold without latch
    wide to a blinding swell of sea?
And Miss Rivera again watches space contract to *this*!
Space like a claustrophobic fist
That gripped her a decade ago
And holds her—*so*!
When *this* has got you
    —and you cannot rebegin—

You have to take it on the chin!
And she fidgets with her costume jewelry
As flamboyant as a poster for a brewery,
And sighing, soon forgets to sigh

> *—in thought removed*
> *and in another place,*
> *the altar candle-light upon her face,*
> *and she as pale as her communion clothes . . .*

And an official, munching apples,
Slaps a dreary youth upon the back,
Assuring him, "The job is gone. You are too late!
Be here next week. Don't let ambition flag, but wait,"
And vanishes into Nirvanas of officialdom
Within a further room,
Whence issues the rapacious ticking of a clock
The youth can hear, as it consumes the wasted hours.
He thirsts for beer. The Carib clutches tight his Rosary

> *—and silver wind blows stunningly*
> *in a raft's sail,*
> *and naked feet on wet, lashed logs*
> *are agile as a frog's,*
> *as morning trumpets from the water-spout*
> *and fish that greet it leap about*
> *among the bland, slow waves . . .*

And a portly clerk in glasses
Genuflects to three fat asses
In conclave by a cuspidor,
Who spit with sated worldliness,
Since they have seen it all before,
Have run for city posts,
And presently, will run once more . . .

> *—and a freighter,*
> *creeping around Battery Point,*
> *blasts the doomed evening*
> *with a sorrowful, judicial horn,*
> *shaking from apathy*
> *the wandering forlorn in Battery Park . . .*

the fog is ripped
and constellations faint and far
slip through
from vistas unattainably remote and blue . . .
The Carib looks about in innocent amaze,
And starting, mutters, in adoring craze;
And Miss Rivera, with abruptly heightened fear,
Surmises how long the foreign nut's been out — and queer!
And in her deep, strange pain in being here,
She steels herself with a last cigarette,
And tip-toes to the fountain
To imbibe from a new, sterile paper cup.
She has to keep herself alive!
She does her stuff in cabaret at five
And she has cooled her heels since one.
But there's no use kicking!
Yes, the Carib is now weeping openly . . .

"That fellow has been up the river,
Ruined himself exactly as at first,
And hasn't either hat or overcoat!"
An entering clerk explodes,
With belly-laughter testifying to his rational doctrine.
"You can't convince the fool his praying is a total loss,
He hangs on, anyhow, to his damn Cross!
I hope, sister, you have common sense.
Some folks like you have fantasies I call immense."

And though Miss Rivera cautiously declines to speak,
And merely nods,
The clerk detects her perfume reek,
And recognizes Woman,
Despite intervening acres of red-tape,
While she, with melting glance and stony brain,
Confronts familiarly, in mood insane,
The Ape in Man . . .

and if the whitening glimmer on dark water
is as constant as the grief man brought her,
thus does splendid night
beget all light . . .

PORTRAIT IN A CAFETERIA
— 1 9 4 0 —

Old man, the past forever at your throat,
You ache with knowledge you will never state
Of griefs and joys beyond you to translate:
Your pulse beats now upon a muted note,
And grimly you refuse to speculate,
Seeing, in death ahead, deceitful fate,
The single certainty in worlds afloat.

You think it cannot matter what you say,
And fix your feet upon the stoic's way:
Cast from you are opinionated speech,
And dreams, once fiery texts from which to preach!
Still flaming anguish at your bitter core,
Rejecting *this*, insists again on *more*.

SHE DIES
— TO MY MOTHER, MAUD THOMAS DUNN, DIED 1940 —
— 1 9 4 0 —

Stunned looks of patience have recast this face:
The brow is stern, serene, augustly high,
Remolding from exhausted commonplace
The setting for the visionary eye
That dimly and aloofly scans this race
It loves no more;—these lips forebear to lie!

These fever-breathing nostrils scent the grace,
The air, the cold nobility of sky!

The travail of the years still mounts, until
This bitter mouth is hers who drinks her fill,
At last, and drains a goblet of pure snow:
The glance acknowledging the end too slow,
Unfathomable, like the moon's clear stare,
Making her pillow terrible and fair.

TO LOLA RIDGE: POET
—DIED, 1942—

Celestial mariners whose stars none see
Must ponder mortals as you meditated me.
Gay and unasking giver, ill yet strong,
Nun-lover of the earth, aloof yet warm,
Child-sage whose spirit was immunity to harm.
No furtive pang of loneliness could lure to lies
A heart that knew no grudging mood,
A mind that, with chaste, sweet solicitude,
Bestowed its insights, burningly precise and pure.
Too frank for consort with evasive meek,
Her wisdom's feast was spread on wayside stone
And ripped by many a harpy beak.
She embraced simply sorrow's taste of iron . . .

Her eyes, so lucent, luminous and grave,
Still out-gaze time and change,
Their gallantry eternal:
The eyes of vision, steadfast, brave!
Such valiant eyes—the very eyes of Good!

MANY MANSIONS
(TO MY GRANDFATHER, THE LATE OLIVER MILO DUNN,
BORN TERRE HAUTE, DIED NEW ORLEANS, 1922)
—1941—

My Father's house is starry with a vernal frost
And brims with sounds of prayer;
Its aisles like stone-wreathed paths
Along a sacred wood,
Evoking, as the autumn fades into November's drear,
Memories of the graves of the forgotten good;
And I recall again—how late!—
An old man, selfless, reticent and kind,
And do not find his homespun ghost amiss
Amidst a worshipped host
Companioned by the glories of the Papal State,
Since he, no less than these,
Withstood the world's betrayals, judged not others,
And yet judged himself with an inexorably clear mind.

WHAT BOURNE?
—1937—

1

O, illusion of self adored in another,
Was myself the moment of love given—
The man loved, child loved, the mother, father, friend?
Has what I am now been wrenched from my flesh?
Is it I, bleeding, I tear up by its roots
From the ancient soil of the past,
With a wail of stricken senses,
Mine, yet mine no longer?

2

Wind of the morning,
Rippling over the city roofs to the sea,
Where dark salt fountains spurt and break,
O, slake the thirsts of this mortality!
Sweep us away
From sight of house-tops, streets and throngs,
To solitary shores
Where rugged rock withstands the shock
Of marbled, silvering attacks,
As quaking mountains pile their snowy racks
Upon ineffable graves!

Let us enter nothing, not as meager bones and dust,
But by spending ourselves upon annihilation generously,
Like the turbulent, terrible waves!
Here hope frets us to extinction:
Better to be tossed, torn, rent with blows
That wrest apart submissive mind and heart!
These are not living whom mere ignominy saves!

3

Snow only adumbrates a further purity,
However sable night,
Beyond it, deeper nights abound.
We have exceeded our tensed senses
And detect a note more remote than the bat's cry,
Yet it may prove but the Cosmic hush
Ascending, as before, from horrible, familiar ground.

PART II

1

Street

To us who had sought long
For prophecy or song
To mute the mutter of machines,
There came,
In the small silence of an empty street,
A bird note! It was sweet!
And there flowed in upon us, once again, that day,
A breath from wide, green living lands
A million miles and years away . . .

2

Neighborhood

The lineaments of dark
Were in the blue;
The windows leaped forth,
Lighted to an angrier hue.
Folk chattered, screamed and shouted,
The radios blared stertorously.
Dogs barked with irritation,
Cats complained, off-key,
Cars blasted canyon streets with sound,
As overhead, in a pellucid wilderness,
The ignored stars began to ripen.

Conniving, secret, all below—
But there above,
Midst roiling snow,
Lay open,
Bare as your own hand,
The mystery no man can understand!

DEUS EX MACHINA
—1939—

Devouring darkness frets the fields,
A crack like lightning sunders heaven,
The mountains rock and sway and shake
With bodings worse than an earthquake.

This trembling glow in which the dead
Grope from their graves
Like folk aroused from bed
Greets the strange quenching of the Star.
The cattle gallop from their barns and low afar,
And birds like mice are flittering in panic-ecstasy.
A cock crows thrice! But wise men,
Stumbling forth to scan the sky,
Learn from it only what the storm-racks tell of rain.

Not yet such solace! Grain bends, pale and bleak,
Upon a tide of drought,
And harrying sand blows from the desert south,
Until the land upheaves into a whirling sea,
And poor folk, fleeing things more dreadful than their poverty,
In wind-threshed rags, seek, with shrill cries, in vain,
For shelter on the tossed and vacant plain
Where man returns to beast,
And camels in the caravan that brings the bridegroom
To the wedding-feast

Cavort and snarl with lions' roars,
And tent-props crash,
And the meek ember of the nomad's fire
Sinks into ash;
While flocks, like drifting snowfalls, bleat
And the shepherd who forgets the wandering lamb
Beats his bare breast,
And peering into space like soot,
Watches the spinning thorn-bush
Upflung, bleeding, from its mangled root,
As by the shattered manger,
Mary searches for her Child,
And Joseph laments mortal grief
The Unknown Friend, so mighty and so terrible,
Can never mend, since all now blindly die
As they were blindly born . . .

At last, the morning!
The sun rises late,
And shines down searingly
On vomitings of hate—
On factory monoliths and city towers!

CITY, AWAKEN!
—1940—

We have forgotten the young moon's thready gleam
Across the mild, starred dusk.
We have forgotten ripened autumn
When the harvest's symbol waxes round and warm
Above the evening quiet of each farm
Where cattle stand in leafy rust,
Amidst haze risen from the tempered dust
Of our mortality.

We have forgotten—
As from springs of gall gone bitter and half-dry
We drink, with metal lips awry,
Our wormwood and asafoetida,
And ever-traveled roads resound
With joyless animation less than life,
While calloused multitudes still pound
The swards of artifice on leaden feet.
There are left to us these lees of sorrow,
Yet we give no look toward welcoming ground.
Such stridence is our anodyne.

Break heart and open iron eye,
And let disorder's human cry
Bespeak the flesh, the earth, the sky!
Sinews grown taut as laboring steel
Regain no pliancy upon the rack and wheel;
There nerves that flex no longer feel.
We are the dead who are about to die!

O, weep! Let tears reflecting blue
Restore to heaven its candid hue,
That numbered coins be laid no more
Upon the drugged lids of futility.

ESCAPE FROM INDUSTRY: JONES BEACH, 1940

The misery of the hour was such
As could not cure itself except with long sleep.
The neon signs had usurped day's departed sun;
Their swift reflections crashed the water's floor
Like bright discharges from a silent gun,
And stars delivered to electric light
Were eyes that blink because they see no more.

Then dusk's deliberation became tide,
Unraveling lines of white about our naked feet,
And as we plunged, deep dark on breast,
We struck out neither east nor west
Upon a current of cold ecstasy:
Before us, sky, so splendidly immutable,
Behind us, land —

> *the changing land*
> *that sank away,*
> *already yielding*
> *in unnoticed sand!*

Yet even at a quarter-mile from shore
We caught a *husha-husha* sound

> *traveling,*
> *lost . . .*

And as the night grew rankly still,
There rose from it
The pulse-beat of a living will—
At last! . . .

APOSTASY
—1942—

Let us sing unto the Lord
And perhaps he will hear us, small
And like the hum of gnats though is the call,
Through over-audible Creation,
Of souls at prayer, from whom is wrung the Word.
Come, Thought, and with an angel's sword
Annihilate the reenactors of man's fall!
Save the new-born! Cut the bloody cord!
The Lord is in his Holy Temple—
Lo, the sterile throbbing of the dynamo
Has drowned the varied human voice!
Duplicity has slain the age,

And now, like bee and ant in muted drill,
The sycophant and dullard erect hive and hill,
Their unanimity mere ignorance of choice.
Industrious parasites have led the way
And invade nature and insult the day,
While Golom's hypocrites beguile the silenced multitudes,
With hope of Heaven to be attained
By methods subtle, vile,
And debased Christians supplicate their Molochs.

But rust creeps in that will corrode
These hearts that love their steel abode.
Machines must hasten with their song
Lest chaos' reign be over-long:
Time can build only on the free,
Strong in the spirit's liberty.

OPUS TEN BILLION
—1938—

If I could build me an arc in the blue
Where the sounds of the city fly under
Like lost birds screaming through a dark forest—
If I could dream again!

But the thought of purity is dire,
And we who would flourish as eagles
Are punished . . .
We cannot, like Ulysses,
Follow yonder star in its fleece
To a home at the end of our days:
Twilights are forbidden us,
And we search the fragments left us
—search like dustmen turning over rubbish—
For the remnants of our silences

And the thought discarded
That was to make a new world.
And if we find a jewel in this offal,
We hide it in our bosom,
Where, though it blaze bright and cold as Venus,
It burns us like a sore.
For the pride that was to be the staff of our years
Bends like some rubber bludgeon
And is a poor defense . . .

Yet as we breathe bitter space
And scent its snowfalls,
Maybe the companioning night will lift us up,
And the grief corroding us
Will twist our veins into knots of iron,
And the anger of our dying
Strip rot from our carcasses as with flame.

Let us be deliberate, O, gods!
Let intention be writ upon our foreheads!
Our births were taken out of our hands—
Let us gird ourselves for death
Knowingly! . . .

THE EVENING CAME
—1941—

The light along the grass grew still
As if the world had lost its will.
Each leaf and bough was painted bright
And yet seemed touched with night.
The land was emptying of day,
And where the living were,
The life of everything was far away.
God's last look on the world

Was like a mighty flag unfurled,
Then joy in all creation died,
And evening crept on us and cried
Like a child who weeps as it sleeps,
Or like a soul bereft of Grace,
And anguished for the morning's unimpassioned face.

LOST WORLD: THE FIRST DEFEAT
—1937—

I have been lonely, I have been among men.
Now, stammering, I try to speak to God again.

Slow Time, the python-strangler of the heart,
Has crushed this thought to dust.
My senses have been shed as husk,
Where was life here? What joy, what bane,
Stirred in me grandeur that ennobled death?
What made of the very transience of my breath
A paradoxical sublimity?

Wound me, lash me,
That I may be mad who am too sane,
And see our midnight
Only by the cold illumination of abstractive brain!
Belief was in the blood—the blood full of crimes!
The veins of the old are like split peas after drought,
And ashes and dust is the word in their mouth.
The old are delusion consummate,
Rebuking youth, since in them is its fate!

O, God, who began granite
From whom eons roll away
Until all being is a day—
Say why the generations are new-born

To question and to end as we,
Forlorn? ...
We would not be as when folk coaxed forth spring with charms,
Saw centaurs and heard mermaids sing.
We reject oracles, divine no more in cryptic runes,
Consult no alchemist, no spell of witch by sea-ruled dunes;
Yet flesh ignored is not renounced,
And merely drops into unexorcised decay.

Let us outdistance desecration!
Let us, who are the voiceless, celebrate the spirit's wakening,
And rededicate the mystery around us
Who are but textbooks on matter,
Whose mathematics multiply extinctions!
O, God, we ask that when they seek us in the morning
And we are not there,
We may be everywhere ...

ENNUI
—1933—

1

The world has gone pale and old
Under its film of gold:
The world, having lost its roots in me,
Is matter now ...
Not a bush, not a taut bough,
But feels the frigid, abstract breath.
Beneath a brassy ray,
The withered fields turn grey,
The snow upon them shaped for stale footprints only.
This numbed purity of unstained blue
Is too impersonal a hue.
To the young, love be the most,

For the rest is tepid boast!
Long lives pass in the fear of hunger
And of death . . .

2

In purple fathoms
Where the eyeless ones turn timid
And retreat,
There are . . .

Gentlemen and ladies
Petal-picking teeth from skulls,
Hairs from corpses . . .
   —*he loves me,*
    he loves me not,
    he loves me not—
The sea is a decorative theme for painters,
And on Sundays,
Religion is an afterthought to roast and dessert.

Does Marx know what it is like
Under the terror whitening the beaches,
Under the dread widening the skies?
   —*there are, beside, the Communists!*—
Speak to the silver-fringed
Whose blood runs cold!
Talk to them about Russia!
They will answer swiftly, silently
From the forbidden deeps.

3

Those white gates are still wide
In invitation:
There lies the way of peace,

Up the pure path spread
From garret to mountain-top.
Among extinct craters,
Birds of Paradise still flutter icy wings.
Yes, age is mild and cold.

4

A generation of lovers forgets hunger,
And a hungry generation scoffs at its own loves,
Yet hunger fed grows again into hunger unappeased,
And from the sating of one drunken want
Spring a thousand new appetites.
So is freedom built with the crust
That, once devoured,
Supplies strength for fresh enslavements!

A SERIOUS PARODY: RETORT TO W. H. AUDEN
—1939—

Though the man with the sheep-dog tramps the wold
And still the heather covers moors with purple elegies,
Britain—they say!—is acquisitive and vile,
Is evil, and—like every evil—old!
Yes, Britain —they say—is crafty and grey,
And the milling thousands swarming over Ludgate Hill
Are puppets propelled by the will
Of feudal lords and grasping bourgeoisie
Who rule the waves far beyond Blackfriars and Waterloo,
And far beyond the draw that lets the red-sailed smacks slip through
The fog, as it steals portions of Tower Bridge.
Upon the Wiltshire plains—they say—the somber druid stones
But mark the sacrifices of a thousand generations' bones;
And in London winters when the Thames is black amidst banked snow,

Men walk in treachery from Billingsgate to Pimlico;
And however often evening settles, like the grapes' bloom,
With deceptive peace, on St. James Park,
We are yet urged to remember Britain's policies are devious and dark!

Big Ben—they tell us—is already set to strike the hour!
And before the blackthorn is in flower,
The very nursemaids will betray us,
As they push the prams along the rhododendron walks
At Kensington and Kew;
And when the Heath grows grand as death
And frosty silence sucks your breath,
We will know Britain's time is done,
And her cathedral spires are toppling upon graves.
Tooting, Euston, Islington, will have to go,
And Nelson on his pediment will be brought low,
And pubs in Stepney will gape desolate,
Unroofed, with genteel boarding-houses around Prince's Gate.
And once muted rumor has begun to creep
To Soho restaurants, the rank tombs at Kensal Green
Will cease to mean what they do now.
And with the deer all fled from Richmond's slopes,
The swans will quit the Serpentine and wing on south,
From reach of famine, gun-fire, pestilence and drought;
For disaster will, by then, have swept the coast,
And as the Wolf and Bishop subside with surf,
So will vanish Britain's might . . .

And the golden bowl will be a sherd,
And from the bosoms of her perished bards
Will spring
A race that cannot sing;
As from Thames to Seine
Begins the desperate reign
Of Reason Absolute—
An eternal end of the pale, damp may . . .

PART III

WAX WORKS
—1939—

Lord Buddha's Wheel, Christ's Sacred Heart
With constellations play their part.
Even Mr. Chamberlain's umbrella
Can affect celestial weather,
As he furls or opens it again,
Though somehow bullets always rain.
Chaos presses upon bourgeois manufactury
And confounds each computation of the careful actuary!
The Gospel Message deep in the financial breast
Insists men sleep, yet none can rest
As Hitler blows the horn of morning,
Hand on hip and forelock leonine
Despite a trembling upper lip.
Blow horn, as every winding height
Is blazoned with immortal light!
This is a music all have heard,
Midst strife the genesis of word!
Sing now the songs already sung
Long before Absalom was hung!
The sun ascending to full noon
Burns mystery from Pharaoh's tomb
And shines delightfully on Franklin D.,
Whose public smile for you and me
Presages reportorial hours
When Mrs. Roosevelt at his heel
Will brood successes like some ardent female seal,
While Stalin ponders with slow cunning thought
Of one whose labors went for naught
Under the Czar, the herds his harsh imagination scant
Prepares, with resolution adamant,

To implement revenge,
And overhead the bloody ball
A billion centuries have not let fall
Rolls onward to the end of destiny,
And up through chill embroideries of space,
Through blankness graven with Creation's face,
The aviators fly, their twenty years
Accustomed to thus rocketing
Above a dwindled hive,
Beheld by them as insignificant and half-alive,
Their joy vacant as they head due west
Into the gardens of the blest Hesperides,
And other lads, familiar with an ocean scene,
Pass over Rubicon in German green,
In an aquatic night they see with crooked eye,
As Hannibal saw Rome grow larger than his sky.
But from ten thousand Greeks,
And from the twenty thousand at Verdun
There rises still, orchestrally, the moan of time,
And of an earth grown colder at its core, aborting rhyme.
There is something here not spoken by those others
Who have split the atom, but who cannot make men brothers.
There is something here for the listening ear
That will outlast the rasping gusts of human fear—
Something for tomorrow to outlast death
In a regathering of all this wasted human breath.

SINCE FREEDOM DIED
—1939—

The space between us and the morning star
Is colder, many times as far
That lucent silver on an empty breast.
Stones upon graves have been piled higher
To make certain the dead will lie as they are.

And might of many, become tyranny of One,
Broods over to assure us dreams are absent
From this dark.
The world that has been with us long
Commands a banquet with a corpse,
And thought, forbidden, has grown false.
Fear, ringing like a bell,
Is all that gives such muteness tongue.
Pens poise to write the verdict—
Let the foolish grieve
That poetry has no reprieve,
The quality of mercy can no more be strained
To meet the natural law
To which compassion is but fecklessness and flaw,
Since the irrational speech of heart
Is disallowed.

But from the idiot's monotony with which it is still said
Men will be men again when they are fed,
We shall yet rally to the whisper of the spirit.
And to the poor who profit in the moment only,
And to the rich who can lose merely what they lack,
Freedom—covert now, beyond the brazen door!—
Will come forth as before
To flower in day's liberal wind.

PURE SCIENCE
(TO DARWIN AND TYNDALL)
—1942—

With broken rudder and on lurching keel,
The Argo you once launched reached promised land:
Your sober dream is vain as scattered sand.
Delusion, treading with Achilles' heel,
Has outrun reason, and where wise men kneel,

Irreverent imprints are the rabble's brand.
Poor pioneers! You trained the ingrate hand
That writes your truth as curse, and yet to feel
The sad, the bitter pang of those who grope
Through labyrinths, to see triumphant Hope
Grin, naked as a skull, and turn to slay
The votaries who paved her blood-slimed way,
Was not the lot of minds that did not swerve,
Or yield, automatized, to rule of nerve!

OUR ERA
—1937—

They have manacled the swallow
And have chained the dove,
And taught the eagle to foreswear his love,
The sky; and mind's flight is no longer high.
Now, since spirit can scarce crawl,
Hope shrinks to dwarf, once proud and tall,
And we press like cattle down a narrow path
And there forget to laugh.
These are the saddest days of all.
Imagination mutely drudges
And what used to be winged fancy merely trudges,
And where sense met intellect on pinnacles of space
The wind blows barrenly
From vacant time and foolish place.
And as the worm, the bat, the tiger
Forage, mate and die,
So I and my diminished race.

APOCALYPSE
—1937—

The moment of the blest had come
When the sun rested like a lion
On the running waves,
And the moon, from her nest of night,
Flew forth with silence like the dove's.
We had waited for this hour
To reach the secret end of ourselves
And go on . . .
It was the beginning, and we knew it
While we went toward death
As children mount a golden stair.
We had never been at home down there!
This light would be the cold white blade
That severed us from our despair,
For now we understood
The strange indifference of the Good.

Though memory followed us a pace
And briefly traced a wound in space,
And Love—always the last to die—
Looked heavenward with a stricken eye,
Above pale garlands spread upon our graves,
Where water joined land to land
In cycles of forgetfulness,
Our hopes, like our fears and lusts,
Had vanished in a flickering, final spark,
And we stood poised upon eternal rims of dark,
So soon would our breath of being cease,
And we become rock, dust, then emptiness—
    The Absolute philosophers dispute!

WAR
—1943—

From dawn-wracked fringes of this void called sky,
Time clamors that a long-beloved face,
A breast that was a blind abiding place,
Be summoned through the needle's narrow eye.
The First Cause dwindles with retiring space,
As it descends from man, to ape, to fly,
Toward our exclusion from the vast embrace
With which abstraction breaks the human tie.

O, earth of rose-crowned, unexpected dawn,
Still pasturing unassisted worm and fawn,
Thankful am I that out of scheming stress
And worlds built harshly upon brute duress,
Can come, despite ambition, struggle, sorrow,
Only the starlight and unmarked tomorrow.

GOOD FRIDAY POEM
—1941—

The sickest hour approaches
When the lewd and grim
Shall seize upon the cream of cruelty
To skim!
Shall scourge him,
Press on him and dote,
The starving wolf within them
About to grip his throat!

They will flay him
As they flay the beast.
Its blood, less precious,
Makes no equal feast!

They will strip him,
Avid to unclothe a god,
That Truth and Mercy,
Beaten down,
May quiver to the rod.

This is the time to nail him high,
Before satiety blunts pleasure!
Lust and avarice, at last, are banqueting
In over-flowing measure!
A sign above will mark him King.
Reserved for sacrifice, and thus alone,
He will compassionate
Where he cannot condone.

Prepared to tender him the sponge,
Their sluggish pulses will no longer creep.
To the delights of torment
Even dullard brains can leap!
Those earth has banished
Turn toward sky,
And were he less
It might be sweet to die.

They thirst! They hunger!
Wickedness is everywhere at stake,
And having read the writing on the wall,
The human spirit they have sworn to break;
While they, his murderers,
Self-accused,
Must needs still fail
With the Perfection
They have ruthlessly abused.

So it will go with Love, again,
Though cravenness, all said,
Abide

By blood and water
From a riven side!

O, Mary, weep
For unseen things and deep.
Such tears,
Wrung through the centuries
From steadfast pure,
Lave blossoms flowering in fortitude,
And these endure.

LAST WORDS
—1937—

I know none of the words I write now
Will be read until I am dead:
The blood will have dried upon them then,
And they will show empty as space,
Reflecting no face.
My cry, resounding hollowly,
Will have been eons lost,
Yet some will lean and leer
And look on this with their familiarly evil eyes
That have pretended to be wise,
And some will seize the rustied pen
And add a line or two
To give the epitaph a proper lurid hue.
But I have written for a few gentle ones
Who are gone,
And let it be if any turn toward me
And my past age,
The dove that is unleashed tonight
Will fly, bright-feathered,
Mild and kind as they,
Up from the darkness of this page . . .

Bleak nursery of souls! The winds arrange
The drifting covers over rotting feet,
As paler spinners mend Perfection's sheet.
How crystal-pure the harvest in this grange,
And yet how steep the glimmering walls of change
Where snow-tamped sockets hold the void they greet!
Though subtle skeins of air are mingling, sweet,
Departure for oblivion is strange . . .

O, graves obscured, will victory still sting
When platitudes of rainfall gently sluice
The clean-stripped bone and earth and sky sign truce?
Will anonymity be roused to sing
A greening ardor in the blades of spring,
Or feel the serpent's fang in verdant juice?

THE THRONG ON CALVARY
—1942—

O, Bright Immortal, now reduced to shade,
The hour when aloof Pilate bent to scan
The victim claimed for sacrifice to man
Draws near again, as fear-drunk millions wade
In shambles about altars. In this glade
Of grief is coursing the same stream that ran
In blood from Paradise. This way began
In Cain! The outcast hand must forge the blade
To pierce your side, the dark heart nail the cross,
The brute force conscience to mourn fatal loss,
Before, defeated, wretched and in pain,
Bereft in spirit call upon the slain,
The many die, and heavy oceans pour
Not tears, but chemicals, on waters dour.

SUMMER STORM

—1943—

Cool seethings move with subtle sheen
Among bewilderments of green:
Fog brings the distance close,
As farthest trees meet, statically, the spell
Of dreamy violence watering hell.
A nebulous encroaching space
Of heavens and storm-wracked earth embrace,
And to illimitable rusty sighing,
Roofs and gutters answer, crying,
With a frantic leap of javelins into air;
And as the walls of empty store-houses, grown thin,
Resound to a primeval din proclaiming flood,
The world takes on the meager color of drab human thought
That goes for naught . . .

And afterward, what awful peace,
As vacantly the downpours cease.
Then trapped like bitter, secret foes,
In ecstasy of rigid woes,
The broken land and swollen sky
Gaze fixedly, each from a stark, bared eye,
And out of rising mist and cloud,
Reweave, once more, a common shroud . . .

TO THE ARTISTS OF EVERY LAND

—A.D. 400, A.D. 1941—

O, desert world, made bleak by fear and hate,
We are your ambushed, who know grief alone,
Like those lost Greeks whose sorrows gnawed the bone
In sea-bright solitudes, while, at the gate,
The Nubian war-cry ordained one blind fate

For all, and withered palms and sky to stone.
The ancient gods decayed, their works were gone:
Again the sands took Silence for a mate.

The painter of the Haz-Awarra school
Resigned, with freedom, the forbidden tool
Of art, and on this frontier of the brain,
The poet, wringing from his lyre his pain,
Heard each star singing, swanlike, through the night,
The proscribed word his pangs released to flight.

THEY KNOW NOT WHAT THEY DO
(FOR CHARLOTTE WILDER)
—1941—

There is a hate born in the tender breast
The brute of sluggish caution never knows:
A gift of hope that hopelessness bestows,
Indriven by the hand that would be blest,
It goads the gentle to a fierce unrest,
Inflaming kindness with a pride that grows
Until abused benignance kindles snows
And crowns the meek heart with a fiery crest.

So on the winds of time is sown the seed
Of dragon's teeth, while force makes mercy bleed.
Mere glut of meat sates mobs protesting wrong,
But not sweet charity that suffers long,
As from wrath nourished by an outraged love,
Years rouse the eagle in the frenzied dove.

BLUE MOON
—1937—

Blue moon, knocking at the window and the open door,
Your surging, storming stillness
Written on the bare boards of my floor,
And on the garden,
Where the ailanthus trees are cowering and dark,
And curse and chatter are flung in from the street,
Your holy threat spreads glacially
Among the blackened trees and to the empty park.

White beacon, shaking down this other-light
From frozen space, upon our tinsel gauds,
Be yet my death-pure refuge,
Signal of Creation's different and unchanging face.

NO BOAST!
—1943—

As prisoners when they toss from side to side
On dungeon straw, exiled from very day,
Still pursue thought's contracting way,—
So we, who see the darkness, like a beast, bestride
The agile reason it can never ride!
Stale oracle dense, cunning council lends
To pettiness for which it ordains shallow ends;
While rabble —fearing great, extolling small—
Dig deep new moats about a wailing wall,
And pray inconstant barricades grow tall,
And nail new Christs upon the Judas-tree
To stop the Voice that, with its softest plea,
Sends mad swine into an Eternal Sea.

Yet gross substantiality is slight
In grip on all it has accounted might!
Beyond cheap triumphs yawns, now, as before,
That ever-open and portentous door
Through which worm will return to worm, again—
No boast of immorality makes men,
But from defeat and grief we will arise,
The brain's clear light our path, our eyes!

LIVE!
—1942—

Pale print of nothing stamps this snowy world;
Enigma leaks from emptiness, and lost
Dusk fumbles insigificance the frost
Subdues. Obliteration's tendrils curled
About dim houses leave their windows purled
And feathered roofs moved, with one shove, almost
Into the void where kindred, love, the ghost
Of thought itself, submit to treason hurled
In white deceit upon an earth agape
For life's defeat and final, subtle rape
By chaos. Little man who will partake
So soon of Lethe, rouse now and awake!
O, nurse the ember! Though its flame be hell,
From it your all, your hope of Heaven as well!

PART IV

SURVIVAL
—1942—

We living have been banished
From the fish-cold wonders of the plan
To serve the lusting brute and slay the man,
And yet we dare to scan askance
An age apotheosized as it counts
Its angels, not on needle-points,
But upon girders, joists and joints,
Imprisoning nature in an empty span.
For caught within these metal toils
Is something false perfection cannot render *nil*!
Mute as Laocöon in these steely coils,
It proves itself in silence, still,
And even as these ugly times despoil the heart,
Bespeaks Creation, *Will*!

POOR CALIBAN
—1943—

Last month the west was like a vacant gate,
And nowhere loomed beyond the mangling glow
The shoddy shopfronts spilled on trampled snow
In streets gripped by constricting cold like hate.
The dark was deep as Stygian nights await:
Warm color had not yet begun to flow
Upon lands blenched by winter, war and woe,
And time's tides seemed forever turned too late.

Life was with human joys and griefs at odds,
And poetry met nemesis in graves.
Now small folk are again content as when
Nature was greater than o'erweening men,
Though Christ's pale footprint on the somber waves
Alone survives a massacre of gods.

ARCHAIC ART
—1940—

Sea-shell, iridescent,
Flushed inwardly with pink,
Plucked from the brink
Of salt and terrible infinity:
I hold you to my ear
And hear an empty roar.
Never will there be more than this!

Glossed feather,
Azured by the sky
Plumed in high soaring
And impressed on your symmetry,
I try with all my might
To grasp impulsive flight . . .
No urgency responds within.

Pure crystal,
Form outliving race
In a museum case,
In bright, mathematical austerity:
The abstract of my thought
But simulates perfection wrought
Ever, by incommunicable earth.

Philosophy
Of alienated mind,
Divorced from natural kind
And primal sources of thought's intricacy,
Builds, on a shrinking shore,
About a vacant core,
Temples never to be filled,

While Reason,
Like a suicide
Become Destruction's bride,
Married to chaos secretly,
Views frightfully, alone,
An enigmatic home,
Walls toppling to oblivion . . .

Frail feeling,
Grapples morbidly with rigorous brain,
As Abel strove with Cain,
To retrieve lost simplicity:
And constantly cries out in art,
From a despoiled heart,
Illusion's ceaseless harmony of dream.

Thus, Being
Exiled from your living origin,
Creation's labors rebegin:
Fastidious intelligence
Evolving will's design
From passions now no longer thine,
But newly springing from life's buried tree.

CONVOY OF 1944 RECOLLECTED
—1955—

Two weeks out of New York,
A moment came not to be staled by anguish,
When from water and stunning isolation,
Where battleship and hospital-ship
Alone kept open pace with the solitary troop-ship,
There emerged, as on the last Day,
From the rain-sooted torrent of sunset horizon,
Sail and funnel, streamline and tanker,
To possess, like ghosts sped from eons of shipping,
The colossus of empty ocean and wave.
And as the dying blaze on the sea
Became populous with a suddenly-revealed host,
What stood forth to us silently
Was as wonderful
As though the napkin laid over the Grail had been lifted;
And again we saw Power benign,
Even as in the dreams of the most ancient of mankind.
But with nightfall,
The fleet dropped behind
Into the smoky blue of stars and darkness,
In which lurked,
Beyond this final mirage of mariners,
Ten thousand years of Power betrayed . . .

THE NEW CITY IN RAIN
—1955—

A sunken shaft of starlight marks each lamp,
Each bridge becomes a circlet of bright thorn,
As cars trail blood-drops round the city's horn,
And evening nebulously fades in damp.
The search-beam rocks above the night's dim swamp,

Now grown the lovelier for being lorn,
Where trembling rays, of crude refulgence shorn,
Brush the black docks, the liner, tug and tramp:
These phosphorescent tails like glinting whips
Great jellyfish throw about port-held ships,
While from more lonely land the quiet juts
In darkness, and the flashing door wind shuts,
Opens and shuts, again, on recalled pain,
Whence we arise from hell into clear rain.

PAGAN INVOCATION TO THE VIRGIN
—1941—

Lampshine on asphalt swept by nimble snow
Turns streets to water with a troubled face:
A heckling angel speeds from place to place,
Dark thought, and windy flakes rush to and fro.
The flagellating storm has brought all low,
And dim day flees tormentedly a chase
By cold, outlawing men and all man's race:
Mere shades and wraiths survive this blow.

Yet with full morning, ocean's very waste
Becomes a mirror just to sky and breeze;
The air grows clement, the sun waxes bold,
And in an amplitude serenely chaste,
A Mystic Rose unfolds among bare trees,
Where are built Towers of Ivory and Gold.

PEACE PACT
—1941—

Through phantom Eden's cloud-wrought gate,
We look past twisted time and place,
Into the stainless sky's awakening face,
At beauty long surrendered and now far.
At last unanguished by pride's flaming scar,
Untouched by restless envy, malice, hate,
In softly startled morning we await
Judgment at nature's great, impartial bar.
Fresh strength is in the ice-pure, crystal wind,
The day is partisan of sober mind;
And sweet as mercy runs the frigid rill
Toward lost horizons and that distant hill
Of philosophic paths none shall dare close
Until have been proscribed the leaf and rose.

TOWARD HOME!
—1942—

As slowly, upon every lifting height,
Stand forth odd symmetries of rock and shale,
Down gilded valleys flows the fragrant gale,
And the ascending, many-petaled light
Again accords the mind the gift of sight;
While ponderings, by multitudes made stale,
Elude the blight of the repeated tale
And wrest from commonplace the unique right
To lands Villon, Verlaine and Heine knew.
Midst basking fields, all silver-sleek with dew,
Keats's batter'd casement is flung wide
On recent battle-ground and blood-soaked tide.
Alas, for ancient, chartless fairy foam—
How like a stranger's is our road toward home!

TO THE MOCKED ROMANTICS

—1955—

1

Your words, like dauntless, rushing pinions spread,
Still thunder dread,
And verity's relentless beams
Show every mountain height aghast and white,
As hosts like hail
With soaring thought and comet-locks
Ignite the gale.
Your stern and magisterial kiss
Is on the forehead of despair, Austere;
And we, with wonder-stricken sight,
Turn restively in our comfortless bed
Toward adumbrations of a withheld bliss.
You bring the magnanimity of space
Into this narrow place.
Descend your radiant armadas,
Smite the false with true,
Ere reason wither to that blindest root
Uniting man with brute,
And Silence answer questioning
With bone-cold lips.
Chaste hearts and intellects,
Offset the savagery of natural law.
May snowy flails beat back the dark,
And poetry become our Ark.

2

The profound stream is turbid, muddied, roiled,
Its font in an exacerbated wound
And fed with blood that wells from many a mound
Where lie those tyranny long since despoiled.

But while new hatreds leave its course turmoiled,
The suffering it floods is like known ground
Through which it sweeps toward freedom with a sound
As secret as the gift it bears, unsoiled,
Upon its breast: a thing greed reckons lost,
And will until some contemplative eye
Descries unransomed treasure's limpid ghost:
The pearl for which the generations die,
Shining from tranquil depths, unflawed and clear
As spirit not to be defiled by fear.

PANTHEIST'S PAEAN
—1941—

The holy dawn,
In ice-blue ecstasy,
Is clamoring in me!
Though the wind move the tree
To the rage of the storm,
And the leaf's flight is wild,
Like the joy of the child
Is my thrill to the might that is free
Yet bound:
Its laws resounding
In the beat of the empty sea,
Traced in the poet's destiny,
The crystal's pattern and the clod!

O, let us,
On arousing to the daybreak's sweet disaster,
Give obeisance to man's natural master.
This shocked enchantment,
Frigid smell of brine,
And radiance climbing
Like a rosy vine, from gushing shadow,

Have provoked me to such gladness
That my heart and mind
—no less than lion and lamb!—
Exult contentedly, in gratitude,
I am! I am!
And marking, in a plume of surf along the shore,
The strand of Paradise,
And in pellucid depths above,
The Lake of Heaven,
Ask nothing more than to participate
In an accord
Like the hushed praise of the Jews' Lord.

A boat glides by on ruffling keel,
And surely beasts and creatures kneel,
As Light speaks, stilly and unheard,
The strangely simple, lucent Word
Of Order, silent and immense.
O, Liberate Omnipotence,
Could I, I would but live and die
In Thy serene and awful Eye;
Guided like cloud and wave on water,
I would again become Creation's daughter.

PREVIOUSLY UNCOLLECTED POEMS

FEAR

My soul leaps up at a sound.
What is the question I cannot answer,
That must be answered?
What is the blank face I must fill in with features?

My brain pulls, stretches, tears;
But I cannot open wide enough to see!
Always at the agonized point of conception,
But never conceiving.
Always giving birth,
But never born!
What is it I am to conceive?
To what must I give birth?

TO A BLIND NAZARENE
(HELEN KELLER)

Secure in blind and perfect night,
And freed from the distress of light,
As deep in inward darkness
I have often longed to be;
As an undivulgèd sea,
When, with no coast to hedge
Scarred silence, slipping gray,
The one breath, on isolation,
Sinks with the coral tendrils of the spray.

End me! I have thought.
Let my mind be still!
Carry me beyond a ravaging by sight,
Beyond an onslaught, made by things beheld,
On muted will.
If I were all my world,

The rays of morning stars would never lash my eyes,
To wake to agony and life a stolid breast.
Sun, crashing its amber on the blazed horizons,
Would stir in me no more than the reflection
On an unplumbed water
Of far, bright unrest.

Then you, with your virgin senses,
Seeing that which you have never seen,
Showed me, as you were sinless Jesus,
Knowing sin and suffering,
Something ruthless vision ought to mean.

CHASTITY

Barley fields are in flower.
White clouds dim a green lake.
The wheat is subtle with silence.
Corn is a forest with silken leaves.
Stone mountains rest lightly
On the pale sea of the sky.
Pines spread loving shadows.
Poplars spend delicate brilliance
On every wind.
Spruces in dour mantles
Harbor the bright-eyed, the fragile of wing,
And those of glossy fur and stealthy ways:
All the creatures of this world
Hungering, thirsting, copulating,
Each small lust and abandon fierce
As that of man in cities,
Committing sin for his daily bread.
In the beginning,
Learning of these cruelties,
I was bound to the earth

By a dear contempt,
The virtue of flesh,
Astounding me,
Has given me another knowledge.
Yet all this, I who die
Must put away—
If not today, tomorrow,
I would have this departure clean.
I would have no descendants.

Three Author's Forewords to the 1948–49 version
of *The Gravestones Wept*

1.

The poems in this book are arranged in consistence with their emotional
content, and not chronologically; but as most of them represent reactions
to circumstances which were either those imposed by military war, or its
precipitants, I have dated them as a matter of possible documentary inter-
est to those less actively involved than I happen to have been in the war and
its preliminaries.

The poems in Part III of *The Gravestones Wept* may surprise readers of
my earlier books, because of the religious note struck; which had its incep-
tion in my "conversion" to Roman Catholicism, in the war's initial stages;
when I was, for a while, in the States, and my husband was in Britain serv-
ing in the R.A.F., and when, also, we were both in Canada, where I was
baptized into the Roman Catholic Church, near the station to which he had
been posted for R.A.F. duty. And though I am now publicly retracting in
the prose work I am writing the profession of faith I made in 1941, because
it is unsatisfactory to my own conscience, I include for their intrinsic worth
as poetry the poems written under a religious influence.

My "conversion" was sincere; and I continue to hold in high regard some
of the Catholics who encouraged my sympathy for certain aspects of archa-
ic Catholic tradition, which I will always admire. But I have, since, been
convinced I would never have been persuaded to attempt a conformity in
religion at odds with the indelible imprint upon me of a Protestant Epis-
copal rearing, and an agnostic and skeptical youth, and with the need for
complete freedom of intellect inalienably one with my character, had it not
been for the artificial conditions which were war's concomitants. And
though my full "apologia" for my own deludedness of the moment is not
set forth here, but elsewhere, I consider it appropriate to mention these

facts, in order to preclude any misapprehension on the part of the public or the Catholic Church regarding my present position, and any misconstruction of the significance of the religious poetry herewith.

As I compiled this book (which is the poetical accretion of years, as I do not write poetry frequently, but "only when the spirit moves me") I perceived, in the poems that, in a measure, reflect a Catholic surrounding, a degree of the "heretical" in my "theology" of which I was imperfectly aware, at the time, and have realized with greater clarity since voluntarily quitting the Catholic Church, for reasons not unlike those responsible for my original relinquishment of Protestant doctrines.

With the exception of the "Good Friday" poem, and perhaps the poem about "Angels," I would seem to have been celebrating a sort of Deistic Pantheism, rather than Christianity pure; this a consequence of an emotionally arbitrary decision to reconcile the Jesus of the "New Testament" and, also, the "Jehovah" depicted by the Jewish authors of the "Old Testament," with the "God of Nature."

I did not succeed in reconciling what to me are still "three Gods," all opposed; because, when under an illusion that I was about to do so, my intellect and critical detachment (though I made every effort to draw on such resources as are mine) were more in abeyance than I thought. And though I acknowledge a debt to my experience, in a certain enrichment of my own insights, I am not persuaded that theologians generally (and particularly purveyors of the "modern") have effected with any greater authenticity, what I found beyond me.

Evelyn Scott, London, January 23, 1949

2.

The poems in this book are arranged in consistence with their emotional content, and not chronologically; but as most of them represent reactions to circumstances which were imposed either directly, by military war, or by its precipitants, I have dated them, as a matter of possible documentary interest to those less actively involved than myself and my husband happen to have been, in the last war and its preliminaries.

The poems in "Part III" of *The Gravestones Wept* may surprise readers of my earlier books because of the religious note struck. But this had its inception in my "conversion" to Roman Catholicism, in the war's initial stages, when I was, for a while, in the States, and my husband was in Britain, serving in the R.A.F.; and when, also, we were both in Canada, near the station to which he had been posted for R.A.F. duty. And though I here publicly retract the "profession of Faith" I made in 1941 (and shall, again, allude to this retraction in the foreword of the novel which I am now completing), I include my poems of a religious character, for what I hope is their intrinsic worth as poetry.

My "conversion" was sincere; and I continue to hold in high regard certain of the individual Catholics who encouraged my maintained sympathy for those secrets of the Catholic tradition reflected in the writings of scores of authors of high intellect, from Pascal, to Proust, Duchamel, and Mauriac, Maritain or Chesterton, and, of course, medievally, centuries before that. But I have, since 1941, become convinced I would never have been persuaded to attempt a conformity in religion at odds with the indelible imprint, on me, of my Protestant Episcopal rearing; with my agnostic and skeptical youth; and with (of ultimate importance!) the need for complete freedom of intellect, inalienably one with my character; save for the artificial conditions war imposed. And though I should prefer to attempt elsewhere my full "apologia" for my deludedness of the moment, I consider it appropriate to mention the facts here, in order to preclude any misconstruction of the religious poems, or any misapprehension as to my present stand, on the part of the public or of the Catholic Church.

I do not write poetry glibly, and as a "business"; and this book is the accretion of years; and, by implication, covers many other things experienced by me, since the publication of *Precipitations* and *The Winter Alone* beside my "proselytization." And yet I think to have omitted what I hope are good poems pertinent to so significant an episode in my life would have been shameful; although I perceive, with even greater clarity than hitherto, the degree of the heretical in my "theology," even at the outset.

I quit the Catholic Church (in which I was a Communicant for something under a year), for reasons not unlike those responsible for my eschewing of Protestant doctrines. And with the exception of "Good Friday," "Angels," "Early Mass During Storm," and "Hymn to the Virgin," I would seem to have celebrated my own version of Deistic Pantheism, rather than Christianity per se, and certainly rather than Catholic Christianity, as usually accepted.

I had made an arbitrary decision to reconcile the "God of the New Testament" and the "God of Nature," and thought perhaps I might discover they had a meeting ground in the "Jehovah" of early Judaism. And under the delusion that these three aspects of Deity could be unified in accordance with my conscience, as an individual, I struggled, for a time, to effect my end, with intellect and critical detachment somewhat in abeyance. But if I failed in my intention, so has many a theologian!

And though the book of religious poetry I thought begun will never be written; as temporary as was the "conversion" aforesaid; as emotionally costly to myself; and as practically disadvantagous to both my husband and myself as authors; I owe to it certain enrichments of my own insight. And because John Metcalfe has remained impeccably aloof throughout, such embarrassing consequences as might have followed my induction into the Church and my withdrawal from it, have been public, and not private, and of lesser import than I had feared. And this, last, too, is, I trust, the case with the very good man who baptized me for the second time in my life.

London, April 5th, 1949

3.

The poems in this book are arranged in consistence with their emotional patterning, and not chronologically; but as most of them represent reactions to circumstances which were either those imposed by military war, or its precipitants, I have dated them, as a matter of possible documentary interest to those less actively involved in the war and its preliminaries than I happened to have been, as an American married to a Britisher and living, until 1941, in an ostensibly "neutral" country, which did not actually declare war until I had left it to join my husband in Canada, where he was serving in the R.A.F.

The poems in Part III of *The Gravestones Wept* may surprise readers of my earlier books because of the religious note struck, which had its inception in my "conversion" to Roman Catholicism in the war's initial stages. And though I have now publicly retracted, in the preface of "Escape into Living," the profession of faith I made in 1941, which was unsatisfactory to my own conscience, I include them for their intrinsic worth as expression.

My "conversion" was sincere, and I continue to hold in high regard some of the Catholics who encouraged my sympathy for aspects of Catholic tradition I will always admire; but I have, since, become convinced that I would never have been persuaded to attempt a conformity in religion at odds with the imprint on me of a Protestant Episcopal rearing, an agnostic and skeptical youth, and a need for complete liberty of intellect inalienably one with my character, had it not been for the artificial conditions the war imposed. And though my apologia in full for my own deludedness of the moment is set forth, not here, but in the preface to the novel to which I refer, it is not inappropriate to mention here, as I did not there, that, having as I compiled the present book, more carefully considered what is indicated in my poems, of my reaction to a Catholic surrounding, I see a degree of the heretical in my "theology" of which I was aware with less critical detachment than I am now able to exercise, when I voluntarily quit the Church. With the exception of the "Good Friday" poem, and perhaps the poem about angels, I would seem to have been celebrating a sort of Deistic Pantheism rather than Christianity pure: this the consequence of an emotionally arbitrary decision I had, then, made to reconcile the Christ of the New Testament and the "God of Nature." I did not reconcile them, as my intellect was not included in the "reconciliation"; nor has any theologian I have yet read done better.

Evelyn Scott, London, August 13, 1949

Author's Foreword to the 1951 version of *The Gravestones Wept*

The poems in my two earlier volumes of poetry, *Precipitations* and *The Winter Alone* were written at widely separated intervals, and except that certain of those in *Precipitations* were the fruits of that experience of Brazil I recount in my autobiographical *Escapade* and so have a flavor of the specific tropical locale not paralleled elsewhere, the volumes are as little unified in theme as most collected writings by poets. However, in the instance of *The Gravestones Wept* this is not the case, since—although several were published in American magazines before nineteen-thirty-nine, the greater number are products of the war itself; interwoven as it was, for me, with a concurrent attempt to embrace the Roman Catholic Faith, in which I failed when, after eleven months as a baptized Catholic Communicant, I realized an incipient despair induced by war's preliminaries and concomitants had driven me to have recourse to "wishful thinking."

My second husband, John Metcalfe, the British author, while serving in the R.A.F. during the war, was posted to Kingston, Ontario, Canada, and it was when I joined him there that my baptism into the Roman Church concluded a conversion begun in the States and, at the time, sincere. And though the atmosphere engendered by Catholic ritual and sentiment constituted, for me, at first, an irresistible appeal, within the year, theological dubieties had overwhelmed me, and I saw that I had not waited on full intellectual conviction to solace emotions just then deeply lacerated by the circumstances of strife, and was in danger of surrendering my own purity of thought.

There began in me, then, a struggle between emotional inclination and a more self-examining intelligence, and this persisted for some years, but the decision to renounce uncritical feeling's supremacy in favor of the concordance of feeling with mind, had become unequivocal by the end of the war, and it is now three years since I formally advised Kingston's Archbishop that my withdrawal from the Church is permanent. I had already tried to announce as much in the public prints, but was forbidden an occasion; and I wrote him many pages in exposition of my apparent vacillatingness. And because, in an acknowledgment of my letter signed by his secretary of today, he was quoted as refusing to comment, yet strained my credulity by stating that, when I was baptized, the Church was not apprized of my ever having been divorced, I here assert my right to this public retort to a statement from His Grace that is an affront to my own integrity. And as I did not dream, until I came to England, that religious conversions were becoming wholesale, and that my enemies, the Communists, were already rapidly augmenting priestly "flocks," it also seems to me the barest justice to myself to say something of the disasters that led me to seek a spiritual haven where—I now gather!—there was none, so that the natural result is my reversal of stand.

In remote, pre-war times, New York, like many another city, overflowed with people conversationally obsessed with social theories of every description. And ten years before the war, it had been borne in upon me that the fine arts in that pure version which is self-expressive, were being condemned as "obsolete" and were giving way to purveyors of "functional" credos of machine-age, robot efficiency in which individuality counted as nothing, and that myself and the creative members of my family were likely, soon, to be faced with problems of livelihood, since we were authors and painters by profession and were unanimous in our opposition to a new regime of tyrannical regimentation, its mediums affiliated labor unions and masses controlled by commercial "planners" who proscribed original self-initiated thinking as "introvert" and decreed the termination of man's span—and woman's!—at forty.

I, John Metcalfe, and the elder and the younger masculine Scott, were repeatedly subjected to barrage attacks—some probably having financial repercussions!—from Marxist "dialecticians" who were under the hypnosis of a theory less an enticement to sentiment than the Roman Catholic legend and as replete with pitfalls for intellect. And I opened counter-fire on the Marxists in 1933, in my novel, *Eva Gay*, and as I continued this in *Breathe Upon These Slain* and did not retreat from an exposure of what, to me, are the fallacies of all "modern" social doctrines when it grew evident that I was more than ever "Labor's" butt, these animosities had not abated when—after the publication of *Bread and a Sword*—John Metcalfe returned, in 1939, to England, to renew his 1914 commission in the R.A.F., and I was left in New York to await pending events.

I was then bound, by a 1937 contract from which I am now released by mutual consent and the lapse of time, to write, for Charles Scribner's Sons of New York, an historical novel which necessitated considerable historical research, for which some money had been advanced me. But from the moment I commenced work on this book, I was beset by vicissitudes; and as my husband, at the outset, had been ill and unable to work, my own funds, shortly, were exhausted after I had given a course of lectures and attended, in an advisory capacity, a single "Writer's Conference." And though I had been, for twenty years, a published author well-regarded, I was abruptly unable to amplify my resources, either with private assistance or with help from any of the wealthy "foundations" established in the States; some, initially, to forward culture, but a majority, I now discovered, dedicated or rededicated to the aid of commercially "applied science" and to the support of "educators" largely converts to the "planned living" which facilitates stereotyping.

War regulations did not permit my husband to send me money. My son by my first marriage, Creighton Scott, was, at this time, contending as a painter and novelist with the difficulties which confronted every American artist not complacent toward commercial or labor dictation, and I was almost as much concerned for his career as my own, and I would not have had him do anything financially toward the reunion with my husband in Britain which my husband and myself desired even had he been able to, which *he was not*. So that in any case it was plain that I must finance my own journey to England.

I was eager to do so. However, I am an American citizen, British only by marriage, and the technical neutrality of America would have obliged me to travel circuitously to Italy, then to Portugal and fly to London, and I had sole responsibility for my mother, who had been divorced by my father, on grounds of "desertion" during the 1914–18 war, and had no means whatever. And as war relations, on my arrival in Britain, would have been applicable to me, also, I could not so much as contemplate sailing arrangements until I first accumulated, for her, sufficient funds to cover one of those indefinite periods people here and there already alluded to as the "duration."

I did not have the means! And though, prior to the war, I had been offered opportunities to supplement my income in a number of those ways which handicap creativity, I now became conscious of an intensification of factional hostilities involving the issues of the war, and that these were closing on me doors hitherto open. And notwithstanding that, in 1932, I was awarded a Guggenheim Fellowship, and the late Editor-in-Chief of Charles Scribner's, Maxwell Perkins, exerted himself indefatigably on my behalf, not a penny nor a post could I obtain anywhere. And it was, therefore, in desperate mood that I decided to explore the conflicts I knew had arisen earlier between exponents of the fine arts and newly ascendent advocates of sheer utilitarianism, and write an article on the subject for a popular magazine such as normally eschewed the serious work of Evelyn Scott, but might be persuaded to publish material pertinent in a current political debate.

I proposed this article to the editors of a five-cent American weekly; one of them replied, and my son went with me to interview him, and when he suggested it might be preferable, instead, to write of an equivalent controversy between devotees of "State medicine" and of private medical practice, and encouraged me to proceed with something of this nature by asserting the readiness of his magazine to publish it, my son tendered his services *gratis* as my "assistant" reporter, should he be required, and I inaugurated a quest for data and what turned out to be four months of penuriously interviewing doctors of every persuasion, and, in the single instance in which I did actually requisition my son, of paying, from my own nearly empty pockets, for him to go to Washington D.C. for me, to see doctors who had been recommended as of both opinions in a dispute regarding a "group" medical project, my attention, meanwhile, having been directed to some recent hospital strikes and to the pertinence of inquiring encounters with such loosely connected bodies as the "I.W.W.'s" representatives and the New York "Prison Parole Board."

All this I now perceive to have been futile, and, no doubt, unwise because misinterpreted, and because, although I unearthed little of startling character, after I had exhibited my brief correspondence with the magazine to one or two hospital heads who had tentatively agreed to discuss the strikes, I was shown copies of various Communist weeklies then being published by hospital underlings and circulating among employees and staff, and was even given a few of these periodicals to use as I saw fit; though I was simultaneously adjured, behind closed doors and in extravagant whispers, to remember "medical discretion" and on no account to quote doctors by name.

The job of a reporter had taken me into an unknown sphere, and I was sensible of such contradictoriness in the evident itch of most of the medical [personnel] to reveal these matters and the dramatic air of "secrecy" generally adopted that, at this juncture, I might have abandoned my time-consuming venture, had I not been aware that the magazine often paid two-thousand dollars for important contributions, and had not my mother, in Tennessee, suddenly fallen seriously ill, and so sharpened my dread of leaving her without provision.

I had, I thought, surely earned some emolument already, and should, at least, finish what I had begun; though, when there were intimations, after some of my hospital interviews, that I was being followed—either by "detectives" or union objectors—I became fearful that my published word, thus denied specific corroboration, might be doubted, and to bulwark my own security and not with any intention of publicizing, I went so far as to ask my son to have a photostat taken of a particular weekly which had been merely "loaned" me, but with the same bewilderingly stealthy verbal permission to utilize its content—it was restored to the owner!—as I considered appropriate.

The single fictional ingredient in *Escapade* is the disguise of my parents—both now deceased, and both probably to be regarded, indirectly, as "war victims"—as a non-existent "aunt" and "uncle"; and while my mother and I were no more than superficially "congenial," the attachments formed by early associations are, in my estimate, ineradicable; and because I could not yet lessen her money-plight, my medical pilgrimages were rendered so harrying that my gratitude over-welled to cousins who rescued her and nursed her until I was able, in the spring of 1940, to remove her to the hospital where she died.

I was able to do this much because, in January 1940, after I had suspended the research essential to my historical novel, Mr. Perkins obtained the consent of the firm to the publication, as soon as I could complete it from a synopsis I had, of the first of the "option" novels mentioned in my contract; and for this book—entitled when published the next year, *The Shadow of the Hawk*—I again had money advanced. But as I myself was plodding daily in New York from hospital to hospital, want still stared me in the face, content though I was with my one-room "apartment" on the top floor of a lodging-house in which the inmates seemed quiet and where I was free to set out for England when I could, as no lease was required. And I was perturbed, as well as annoyed, when the Belgian janitor—a clod in temperament but previously deferential and fairly competent—evinced a sudden surliness and informed me, with every appearance of duped conviction, that Britain was "already in the hands of the Nazis," that my husband was "probably a Nazi prisoner" and it was "not likely" I would "ever see him again."

I do not know what prompted these intimidating remarks, but the janitor was a mechanic and had contrived for himself a very good radio, and he may have been stuffed with "haw-haw"discourses of a sort with which the British are familiar; and, in any case, it was impossible, in that winter and spring of 1940, to cover the dial of any radio at all without being bombarded by the rantings either of Communists, Fascists, or "Christian Socialists," or the war-sensationalism of journalists who reveled in the depiction of blood-shed and blood-thirst. And as a woman with a husband in the War Zone, I, shortly, became alarmed, and—acting on the counsel of a legal friend—reported the janitor to the Department of Justice.

It was to be a further year-and-a-half before America, too, became officially belligerent; and my complaint was of intimidation and not of the treason of which, technically, the man was guiltless. But I had no doubt I had done right when, subsequently, my typewriter, which had been in decent, workable condition, was mysteriously nearly demolished over-night and he averred that a marauder must have entered my room at a moment when I was absent and thrown "acid" into it; a view approximated by that of the man who repaired it and who also upset me by declaring that just once before in his life had he ever beheld a machine similarly devastated, and it had been "recently in use in the tropics during a rainy season"! I have spent two winters in the North African desert, but have not visited the real tropics since 1919! Nor were my awakened suspicions of the janitor lulled when he predicted that the property of Americans was soon to be appropriated by the Government and re-divided "equally" among the citizenry, and that I would, shortly, be "lucky" to "earn fifty cents an hour scrubbing floors."

However, my protest against his menacing talk may actually have confounded those responsible for law-and-order; as no apparent notice was taken of my communication to the Department of Justice until the ensuing summer, after I had already removed to Saratoga Springs, to finish *The Shadow of the Hawk* there at the home of a friend. And when, from Saratoga, I replied to the Department's representative telling him of my altered whereabouts, there was no acknowledgment of my letter until the Christmas season; and it was afterward that I was notified that the same representative had "called" at my Saratoga address while my hostess and myself were away, in Ossining, New York, participating in the holiday diversions of a couple who were her friends and were very agreeable, although my own pleasure in the brief sojourn there was diminished by my abrupt feeling of repugnance for the sordidness of American "Law," a distaste heightened by the fact that the town is the site of Sing-Sing Penitentiary, which is its "water-front."

I cannot say whether the accosting of a middle-aged woman by a male "flirt" during an Episcopal Church service is an Ossining commonplace or not; but the male who intruded on me when I went to Church alone seemed to me "planted" behind me to ogle, smirk and offer unsolicited advice on hymn-numbers. And as there was, beside, a further passage with a stranger which hinted of malice, I am yet at a loss to know whether my interchanges with the Department had cross-purpose results that were merely "coincidental," whether these were "tactfully" pre-arranged under an erroneous impression that I was being saved embarrassment, or were the outcome of a deliberate hostility to my British sympathies and so devised that it might appear I myself was somehow in flight when, on the *third* occasion of a Departmental descent, I had, not long before, "vanished" into the wilds of the Kingston R.A.F. Station to delight in the recovery of my husband's society by the duties which had sent him again to the North American continent.

Nonetheless, I resume here my narrative of the lodging-house of the antecedent year, as it was many months prior to the R.A.F.'s dispensation that I dispatched the original version of my medical article to the editorial office which had commissioned it.

I had been scrupulous in my fulfillment of the requests of the interviewed doctors, hospital superintendents, and nurses' organizations not to quote by name; but I had not felt the same hesitation in quoting the already-published and signed opinions of yet other doctors whom I had not approached, and whose views circulated in pamphlets printed by organizations ranging from "The American Medical Association" to the unions. And there were, beside—interspersed throughout my article—excerpts from the Communist weeklies, which the article decried as gratuitously libelous and scurrilous. And I was dashed when the editor who received my script returned it to me at once, with compliments for my achievement in "journalese" but with the fresh request that I delete from it specific mentions of *every* kind and revise it in accommodation to this change.

I had just had news that my mother's case was grave, but I put by *The Shadow of the Hawk*—on which I was no more than launched—and, somewhat sardonically, essayed to do as I was bid. And the second version of my article was mailed to the magazine on the eve of my departure for Tennessee to effect the shift of my mother from the midst of my cousins to a small ward in a building once the home of family-friends and, in part, endowed as a medical hospice by an uncle-in-law who was deceased.

I think my mother was well cared-for, but her position was excruciating in its reminders of a happier era; and as, during my sojourn of three weeks, I watched her die, it sometime seemed to me that I was, also, witnessing the death-throes of the Victorian South, so much hers, though it disgruntled her and she had tried repeatedly to exceed its myopias. And I was harrowed within, though I believe calm without, for she was calm as seldom in her life, and not, except at moments, because of stupor.

But I could not remain with her to the very end as the magazine's check, on which I had been relying, did not arrive, and I could not afford the luxury of protracted grief while, for the first time in my life, in debt to a publisher for books still to be written.

In New York, I discovered my journalistic experiment had been rejected; the magazine having capped irony by commenting that this was because it was now "without enough *human* interest." However, though returned—so say the editors—to the address of the New York friend who had been asked by me to take temporary charge of any mail and forward letters, she and no one else had laid eyes on it, nor has anybody since then, as far as I am aware. And my conjecture that it might have been abstracted from the mail in transit had plausible substantiation in the fact that, at this point, I was already rendered anxious about mail deliveries by the abruptly proclaimed presence in the same postal district of several "Evelyn Scotts," some of whose mail had come to me and obliged me to complain to the Post Office regarding re-addressings.

I was told of an "Evelyn Scott" whose check to "Bundles for Britain" appeared to have been confused with mine; and when I telephoned its office, I was assured she was a "daughter of a patron." An ex-college student of my acquaintance, then employed in a Y.W.C.A. bookshop, told me with amusement of a chocolate-colored book borrower who designated herself, perhaps correctly, "Evelyn Scott." An "Evelyn Scott"—to judge by a postcard I re-directed—was presiding at "literary causeries" in a house on Hudson Street unknown to me. A New York daily probably still has on file the paper which reported a "Bundles for Britain" soirée attended by Mr. and Mrs. Charles Dana Gibson and "Miss Evelyn Scott," among others; and as Mr. and Mrs. Gibson and "Miss Scott" were bracketed together and I had not been of the party, I was perplexed to grasp why, when I had dined, with friends, at the Gibson home a year or two before, they had not referred to any friend by my name. My own medical doctor, on seeing that I had begun to feel disturbed lest this influx of "Evelyn Scotts" occasion the loss of some of my British mail, took the trouble to go to an address given—I think by the Post Office—as that of the "Evelyn Scott" nearest, there to request aid in straightening out an incipient postal tangle. And while my rumored "prototype" was not visible to my emissary, the name, "Evelyn Scott," was with the name of a Jewish lady by the bell of an apartment; and the Jewish lady was seen by my proxy, and introduced herself as an editress in an old New York publishing firm, and affably agreed to make certain that the sharer of her quarters sent on, as a mutual favor, any mail for me misdirected to her.

During my over-twenty-years among New York publishers, I had not heard of the Jewish lady. But more indicative of the war-time transformation of New York was the fact that when I was notified—in the midst of these "distractions"!—that, without my knowledge, I had been "elected a member of 'P.E.N.'" and I decided it advisable to attend at least one "P.E.N." dinner before I left New York, I shortly found myself seated at a table at one of these assemblages beside a Jewish lady presented to me as also of the publishing-house mentioned to the doctor, and this lady—as the dinner guests were about to wend homeward—invited me to take with her a taxi which set her down before an apartment house door where, again— the very next morning as I was passing the place on foot and stopped for an instant to reconnoiter her lobby—I observed "Evelyn Scott" inscribed with a Jewish name by the portal.

I soon ascertained that the apartment visited by my medical friend had been recently vacated, so that there appeared to be small doubt that the "two editresses" were the same woman. But to have said as much to me as she and I were chatting amiably would, it seemed to me, have been the natural thing. And while it may strike by-standers as merely ludicrous that I received, at this time, a race-track program on which an "Evelyn Scott" figured as a track-entrant, I was in no mood to laugh, since the portrait of me by Francis Criss which had been much displayed in New York had, likewise, lately, been whisked from the walls of a friend's living room—by whom, no one knew!—and I had just been the further recipient of a letter from a stranger in which the writer boasted that he had hung my "portrait" with those of his "heroes": the single "hero" to whom he alluded being a German general.

The address on this letter was in the vicinity of "Mecca Temple," a favored rendezvous of "Labor"; and I guessed I had been "let in for" some sort of "Labor" *charivari*, unless—having British connections—I was perhaps under surveillance by an "Army intelligence" of some kind addicted to methods suggesting "madness" to the uninitiate. And when, afterward, in Canada, in the course of my husband's R.A.F. transfer from Kingston to

Clinton, near Lake Huron, there disappeared, as well, the portion of my historical novel I had brought with me in the hope of resuming work on it already delayed because I was not offered access to Kingston's University Library until on the brink of leaving, I did not forget these New York episodes, and wondered if someone cognizant of those events could have taken or destroyed my manuscripts in spite; an act which deprived me finally of any opportunity to carry on with this book until, at the end of our two-years-and-a-half in Canada, my husband was repatriated for service in England and I returned temporarily to the States to see my son and retrieved, from a Saratoga safety-deposit vault, a carbon and notes on my novel which I had been afraid to risk to mails and moves.

However, I was not yet in Canada when the climax was attained in the incidents I now regard as tantamount to that "softening-up" process of war of which I have heard the military speak; and I have still to allude to two Government "investigators" of "W.P.A." "Art Projects" who went to a politically ingenuous and innocent artist friend in "W.P.A." employ to inquire of her whether she knew anything of an "Evelyn Scott" who had "once been" on a "Project" and was thought to be "politically subversive"!

I have never worked on any "W.P.A." "Project," but my first husband was then the Director of an easel-painting project from which, eventually, he resigned because of union interference with his attempt to allot commissions on the basis of merit, and as we all saw him now and again in a friendly way, I realized he was finding his position a trial as he opposed political irrelevancies from every source. But my friend, nonetheless, sent on the "investigators" to me that I myself might dismiss any absurd assumption that might have confounded me with the "subversive."

The "investigators" were not markedly disagreeable, and one visited me twice and continued outwardly amiable. But their incursion did not add to the "joy of living"; especially as my son, too, had once briefly essayed "W.P.A." work in the arts, and, after being highly commended and listed for "honorable mention," had been warned that he must "join the union" or he would "lose his job," which he shortly did; though there was no complaint against him and he was merely told he was a "supernumerary" and "superfluous."

And the fact that I, apparently, was included in an "investigation," at length, so wrought upon me that I confided my woes to a cousin who lived near New York, and she, in turn, introduced me to a friendly conservative Congresswoman whom I asked for advice on some means of ridding myself of such plagues and confusions. And though she herself had none to give, she offered to send on to me a *third* "investigator" with whom she had but slight acquaintance, yet hoped might prove a well-disposed counselor.

The Congresswoman was not, I may say, over-sanguine respecting the value of "investigations" as they were then—and perhaps still are!—conducted; and I became even less an optimist when this particular inquisitor knocked at my door—by appointment, to be sure!—a few hours after there had been left with me the telegram announcing my mother's death, and, though I produced the message in explanation of my probably flustered mein, was not deterred, by my bereavement, from extracting from me whatever she could that bore on her occupation.

She professed to know me by reputation, and she was, indeed, almost affable; but it now seems possible that she believed she had divined in me a "labor informer"; and having begun to put queries to me, she kept hard at it, in her attempt to "get to the bottom" of "subversiveness" in, I presume, my unfortunate person, from either four or five in the afternoon to around nine that night. At this "genial" grilling over, perhaps I should not have been surprised by other descents on the lodging-house of conspicuously "secretive" men wearing badges.

One such influx was proclaimed to be due to a theft of clothing; and in this instance, though I descried "plain-clothes men" in neighboring rooms and was told they were searching every room in the building, my own room was sedulously avoided until—on hearing they had dispersed—I went in some indignation to the nearest police station and succeeded in bringing some sort of policeman back with me to examine my belongings, also, and so forestall the hostile janitor's possible misinterpretation of the ambiguity of an ostensible "considerateness" apparently without motive.

But the day came when the lodging-house was not to be further tolerated, though the alternative be such an apartment as I had rented previously, where Jewish tenants above danced fandangoes as if on my head as I wrote and tenants beneath—said to be Germans—their hours of bed erratic, loudly derogated certain of New York's *literati*—sometimes derided as infamous at the lodging, too!—in loud tones audible sporadically up the living-room chimney. And subsequently, I wished that I had ascertained *before*—and not *after!*—I quit the lodging-house, that the portfolio I had with me there had been, at one stage or another in my progress toward Canada, virtually emptied of my collection of the valuable water-colors of Cyril Kay-Scott, of Creighton Scott, of the late Owen Merton, the British water-colorist, and of some isolated examples of other American water-colorists of high intrinsic worth.

Mr. Kay-Scott, my first husband, and our son were both then exhibiting, and Owen Merton—once a fairly frequent exhibitor in New York—was already hung in the Brooklyn Museum; and the pictures of these three painters were priced at eight-hundred dollars for the best examples by Mr. Kay-Scott—admittedly a great water-colorist—five hundred for the best of the brilliant Mr. Merton and from fifty to a hundred for those of the yet-young Mr. Creighton Scott who was regarded by a number of the older painters as the most promising American painter of his generation. But I had temporarily lost sight of the imperiling of these paintings when irony reached its apex in the detention, at police headquarters, of a professional artist's model with whom I had a decorous bowing acquaintance and who inhabited a room on a lower floor. She was, it eventuated, charged, by "The Society for the Suppression of Vice"—its nearest British counterpart is "The Lord's Day Observance Society"—with having "illegally," notwithstanding her model's license, posed for art photographers. And though she was soon exonerated and released, this was not before more "plain-clothes" men had intruded on a domicile for the moment mine, also, and, with them, a police woman, who began a vigil in a room *not* adjacent to the model's but a few yards from my own, the official presence underscored by the fact that the door was kept ajar.

In the nineteen-twenties, this same "Society" of self-appointed "moral censors" instigated the suppression of *The Rainbow* and *Lady Chatterly's Lover* by the late D. H. Lawrence, and of *Ulysses*, by the late James Joyce: novels which, as we all know, are now classics. And it was while the trial of the publishers of *Ulysses* was pending that I went alone and on my own initiative to importune Mr. George Sumner, the organization's head, to retract his allegation that *Ulysses* is "obscene" and dismiss legal proceedings impoverishing to an artist of exceptional integrity who, already, was poor. And though when face to face with the Comstockian demolisher of realistic masterpieces, I was less struck by intimations of conscious and purposed evil than by symptoms of moral cravenness and of that curiously perverted view of Christianity to which "the flesh" is foul, than by his obvious total lack of aesthetic discrimination, I so notably failed in my mission that, in 1939, nearly twenty years after this futile conclave, I could but regard it as a nadir in implied insult that I myself—however, "fortuitously"!—was subjected to a political surveillance as humiliating as inexcusable.

On my floor of the lodging, there were just two other tenants, both women, and one of them a personal friend who could scarcely have come under suspicion, as she is the daughter of the former Dean of a Michigan University college who was then alive, and is herself the author of some very fine short stories, then responsibly employed as the chief editor of a fashion magazine. And as both these women were absent in offices during working-hours, the policewoman had nothing on which to focus her attention save me and the window overlooking the street. And when, after she had been my neighbor for twenty-four hours, I emerged from a "Rikker's"—where I had breakfasted— in New York's deserted Sunday thoroughfares I realized my footsteps were being dogged by a man who, though he had crossed to the opposite pavement, lagged as I did and accelerated his pace as I walked quickly. I at once resolved to transport myself and my baggage elsewhere on seeing him stop on the corner by the lodging to gesticulate extravagantly with every effect of signaling at me for the policewoman's benefit.

I hastened to the home of my son and his wife; and as they had no extra bed, my son appealed to a friend to house me; and her husband gave his assistance during my son's removal of my trunk and other baggage to the dwelling of the couple, who had already read with consternation a newspaper report of the model's detention which, in publishing her address, published mine in contexts likely to be damaging to the reputation of the establishment.

I was ill from nervous tension and exhaustion. But on bracing myself for the journey with a brief interlude of rest and storing some of my luggage, I traveled to Saratoga, as I have mentioned; arriving there, also, in a state of dilapidation, in consequence of some "finishing touches" to the macabre atmosphere which seemed to envelope me: these in the shape of an impact from a roadside obscenity not debatable to the extent of Mr. Joyce's use of an Anglo-Saxon vocabulary, and from a glimpse of the captioned squib about the model on a news-sheet thrust under my nose by a vendor on the train, who, inscrutably, proffered me a paper already several days old.

These are typical salients in the prelude to my essayed conversion to Catholicism; and as I relate them here, it is for my country, and not myself, that I blush. And in Saratoga, where a visit originally to have been merely of the summer was extended that I might complete *The Shadow of the Hawk*, I was harrowed again in being helplessly obligated to the generosity of a hostess who refused reimbursement for the expense of my prolonged stay when she saw how vainly I seemed to be struggling yet to accumulate my fare to Britain.

As early as 1937, I had been attracted to Catholic literature by the Church's better intellects. And in January, 1941, I petitioned Saratoga's Catholic Seminary for instruction in the Church Catechism. And when my husband, to my utter joy, was posted to Kingston, and—*The Shadow of the Hawk*, at last, in the printer's hands!—I, too, had proceeded to a town divulged to me, on arrival, as the seat of an Archbishopric, I asked that my instruction be resumed. And in Kingston it was continued by the Archbishop's secretary of that period, and was concluded by a private baptismal rite which had one witness other than the officiant.

Such is the literal record of a disaster! But to transmit here, to casual readers, the emotional nuances of the gradual overwhelming of my naturally critical and self-examining mind by elusive factors of feeling stemming both from the war and from my own early life in the South, is beyond me; and I can merely hope that something of this experience is conveyed in certain of the poems in this book; for my mood, briefly, became as naively trusting as when, as a child, my preceptors were the Episcopalians of my orthodox rearing, against whom, in my teens, I rebelled. And though I was still considerably under fifty, so not precisely to be classed as "senile," I was slowly wafted, by almost imperceptible degrees, back into a time when, in New Orleans, long before I met Mr. Kay-Scott, I had been wont romantically—and in the way of adolescence—to court elevation in solitude in the Roman hush of the St. Louis Cathedral, which had, for me then, that flavor of "foreignness" I linked with far horizons into which I had determined to escape, and where I wrongly supposed the crudity, sordidness and pettiness already perceptible to me in a familiar environment would somehow diminish.

No, I do not believe the "Word of Moses" is supernatural "revelation"! No, I do not believe Creation's First Cause humanly embodiable—and least of all in an evilly disposed effigy like "Jehovah"! Neither does Catholic "miracle" hold any appeal for me save as the sum of man's earthly frustrations, in all their pathos, is implicit in Catholic legend. And while Catholics make much of "transubstantiation," had I been challenged to ponder it as "miracle" would have it, I should have been merely revolted by it as a sort of "Divine" cannibalism. To encompass it except as symbol is not within the compass of my imagination, and though I often left the Communion-rail genuinely exalted by an unremitting dwelling on the thought of goodness as pure benignancy, I now realize that these tenets of Catholicism—though among the chief!—had small part in my reflections.

I do not believe in "Jehovah" as the "One God," or in "miracles" or in "transubstantiation," and could never have believed these things with the full concurrence of my mind. And the goodness I re-envisaged diligently from 1937 onward was, again, the same Mr. Kay-Scott and myself discussed philosophically—though he, then, more than I insisted on manifesting it maturely—when preparing, in 1913, to go to Brazil: our flight there, also, as we saw it, an "escape from the world" that impinged on one in which we could sustain each other in spirit.

In 1913, I was inconsistent, doubtless, and in 1941, inconsistent as never before! But as I attempted to reconcile mind and heart, it seemed to me that a creative intellect such as François Mauriac's—for instance—must see the "seven swords" of St. Thérèse somewhat as I did: as symbolizing her wounding by an experience of living that—as to happenings!—does not come to anybody in the form of a prescription, though the prescription be the Pope's own. To "know" Catholicism, I must essay to "live it," I thought!—and who among those who admire the perfect translation of Rainer Maria Rilke's Verkündigung by that pure, lovely and original poet, Charlotte Wilder, can suppose Rilke accepted unqualifiedly religion's common, crass purveyance of the "angel's" visit to the glorified mother?

Was Jacques Maritain satisfied—I wondered, in Canada—to have "God" represented, even to "children of Sunday-School age," by a literal drawing of an "Eye" termed that of "Conscience" and tending, as mere "Eye," to the "diabolic"? And could it be that the warm and outgoing Gilbert K. Chesterton—who, in his lifetime, had astutely forecast totalitarian abominations and deplored them—had lightly discounted every finding of pure science pertinent to time and geological change, as he took religious stock of a Judaical compounding of the "world" in "seven days"?

I could not accredit to a man of Chesterton's wit faith in the mapped location of a possible "Garden of Eden," or in a genealogy of races tracing all of them to an origin in a murderous renegade called "Cain," who, apparently, had been guilty of incest, as, otherwise, he could not have effected "propagation." But in the States and Canada, when among Catholics, I was surrounded by unconscious literalists such as are, I now have no doubt, the body not only of the Catholic Church but of every Church organization invested with that temporal power which is increased in the measure in which it exploits debased versions of originally deep insights, for the governing of people of inferior sensitivity and no perspicacity whatever. And as I wrestled inwardly—all unknown to my "Confessor"—with my speculations on the extent to which I was technically obligated to approach religion as might an Irish or French peasant, my growing bewilderment was accentuated by the signs about me of the militant mistrust with which Canadian Catholics of South Irish ancestry were being scrutinized by Canadian Protestants of North Irish extraction.

To be "above the battle" was, I had supposed, the very *raison d'être* of every Church! But how was I to interpret this when I saw hoodlums, said to be the children of "Orangemen," urge dogs into the Cathedral through the street door during Mass, frolic in Holy Water basins when the building was nearly empty, and heard complaints of the rifling of poor-boxes, and of an illicit "queuing-up" before Confessionals of gamins unconnected with Catholicism?

I myself was annoyed by a carrot-headed contingent who once "booed" at me in the road. And as certain of the wives of the younger officers— markedly uncordial and occasionally really rude, I attributed this, also, to Canada's current feud which had it that Irish-Catholic loyalty was "slightly suspect."

The priest of my baptism—who, as an R.A.F chaplain and, later, the incumbent of a new Church, continued to be my religious advisor—was distant from old Ireland, but it had been the "land of his fathers," as of some of mine; and because he spoke of it with natural sentiment, I abruptly began to find it more than ever arduous to maintain my first complete candor toward this simple and, I think, kindly man; who would be likely, in any event, I thought, to regard the dubieties which had followed so soon on my conversion as "blasphemies" against the "Holy Ghost."

However, I had grown, again, acutely unhappy respecting everything except the consoling proximity of John Metcalfe; who, as I groped for a solution of my problem, was tactfully reticent. And the decision I finally made might have been less belated had I been allowed to clarify my own opinion of a predicament, for me unprecedented, by articulating my metaphysical travail in the expressive medium of the written word that, to every author—as paint and canvas to the painter—is so much tongue and voice that the "thinking-process" cannot be said to conclude, for them, without recourse to its use. But while, in the beginning, my baptizer had encouraged me to hope for this normal procedure, after a single article by me, which treated of metaphysics, was published in Kingston's Catholic weekly, I was rendered, as to print, mute: a condition shortly re-emphasized by the apparent theft of the original manuscript of the historical novel to which

I have alluded. And because, at this juncture, I began to feel I was merely drifting, I made a less whole-hearted effort, after my husband's posting to Clinton, to reorient myself with religion by attending the Anglican Church there, though as an onlooker, and not as a Communicant.

But at the Anglican Church, I was merely re-plunged into the Episcopalianism from which I had broken away in nineteen-seven; and while the vicar and his wife were generously cordial in manner and lavish with gifts of flowers and proffered considerate attentions, when he had avowed himself to be an "Orangeman" to whom Catholics—particularly Irish Catholics!—were a "red rag," and, in addition, some of his parishioners had gossiped of divorce, in my presence, as opprobrious, I was, again, in the plight of one at bay, and recognized the disparities between my view of religion and his as not to be bridged.

And still I was not aware that my status as divorced figured—as I now realize it must have—in the Catholic attitude toward me, until, in London, a few years ago, I received the Archbishop's quoted pronouncement intimating that I had deliberately suppressed an important fact in my life that I might gain comfort from *what?* I had interrogated my Catholic instructor in Kingston very pointedly about divorce, and inquired of him whether a prior divorcement were an obstacle to acceptance into the Church, and his reply was that it was not, as the Church assumed no responsibility for the acts of converts prior to conversion and its religious jurisdiction over marriages concerned only marriages which had taken place under its aegis.

It is true that I did not invite the priest to probe into the details of my first marriage or into my divorce from Mr. Kay-Scott, but I frequently referred to my son and especially referred to him as, also, the son of Mr. Cyril Kay-Scott, the painter. And when I stipulated to the priest that I be *not* required to confess to the specific incidents of my life as "sins" and he consented to allow me to make merely a "General Confession," as it was designated, I supposed he did not press me for information about my divorce through delicacy of feeling and because I had just endured a politically-incited ordeal of which I told him. And I will always find it difficult to grasp how it was possible—if so!—that the Archbishopric, which is in constant contact with New York, was, as is since suggested, unapprized by other lips than mine of the unusual phase in my life recounted in *Escapade* and including the full and actual explanation of the situation which forced Mr. Kay-Scott and myself to establish a Common Law marriage as the one means of legalizing our relationship and the legitimacy of the son who is very dear to us, and who, even so, had, to date, been deprived—by what means we know not—of a share in the estate of my grandfather, who initially proposed to provide for us all.

The nature of my marriage to Mr. Kay-Scott has never been a "secret," nor has the fact of the divorce from me which he obtained on civilized grounds in Chihuahua County, Mexico, and which had the sanction of the American Government in the American Consular signature of the witness to the decree. But there is something about the political mind that contaminates whatever it touches; and as His Grace has evidently misjudged me and perhaps has yet to read Mr. Kay-Scott's autobiography, *Life is too Short*, it seems to me he should know more of the conduct of his own diocese in which—it is plain!—politics are still rife, and that he should be less hasty in imputing evil to people of whose characters as individuals he comprehends nothing—not even the anthropological possibility that they may be idealists whose outlet is in a different *mores*!

My "General Confession" was spontaneously tendered as I contrasted my very human faultiness with the image of Perfection which is Charity's personification, but I was not, as His Grace must know, offering, to him or any other individual Churchman, an apology for any act of my life, and was, indeed, surmounting to an extent and by an effort of willed emotion, the result of a bitter, bitter hurt already imposed on me in Europe by a Catholic priest who, while my son was yet a child, attempted to proselytize him when I was absent from the immediate scene, and proposed, as a basis for this endeavor, that he be permanently separated from a mother so reprehensibly unorthodox that she had better be "accounted dead."

This is veracity! And as I love my son in no abstract sense, I think the Charity I tried to exact of myself in 1941 would eventually, in any case, have proved too much for me. But I still—alas!—labored, then, under the misapprehension that to be a "Christian" was to imitate Christ as nearly as one could; and as I meditated the views of St. Francis of Assisi, of St. Augustine and of St. Thérèse and thought less of those of my Kingston associates, the matter of my divorce appeared to me comparatively insignificant, especially as my second marriage, as well, is civil and could not have been regarded as religiously sanctified.

My conversion is, of course, a "closed chapter" in every Churchly sense, but I am amazed as I consider it retrospectively that the Church omitted to concern itself with the potentialities of so serious a step in relation to their ultimate effect on other lives than my own; and to me—psychologically, emotionally and creatively, as a writer—the "chapter" is no more "closed" than is any experience vital to me. And were Churchly Powers wont to admit their errors as freely as I here admit mine, I would by no means altogether regret my increased conversance with that deep poetry of religion which, in some ways, is at its finest in the Catholic ritual, prayer, and legend. Nor do I acknowledge this out of mere "intellectual vanity," or concede it to signal that "exhibitionism" of which "psychoanalysis" long ago convicted even the saints.

Such a preamble to the reading of a few poems which I, nonetheless, ask to have critically assessed strictly on their own merits, may, to some, seem strange. But the world's common, polite obliviousness to the war's part in episodes of this sort—wracking and harrying though they are to the duped and victimized of all persuasions!—has contributed to the "economic" casting of my lot ever since—and, to a degree, my present husband's, Mr. Kay-Scott's and our son's—with those who are *creatively* as dumb as the brutes, and I seize on this as the first opportunity given me to make my position clear to the friends who are, also, readers of my nineteen published volumes and of the many books by members of my family, who are no more habituated than I to the roles of the creatively silenced.

Evelyn Scott, London 1951

NOTES

The author acknowledges the courtesy of the editors of *The Poetry Journal*; *Others*; *The Egoist* (London); *Poetry: A Magazine Of Verse*; *Playboy*; *The Dial*; *The Liberator*; *Others: An Anthology of the New Verse*; *The Nation* (New York) , and *The Lyric*, from all of which poems in this volume have been reprinted.

p. 5   "Ascension: Autumn Dusk in Central Park." *The Dial* 49 (September 1920): 268.

9   "Midnight" published as "City at Midnight." *Poetry* 15.2 (November 1919): 73.

13   Author's emendation from a personal copy of *Precipitations*, HRHRC Evelyn Scott Collection, EMBARKATION OF>EMBARKATION FOR

13   "Lullaby." *The Poetry Journal* 8 (1918): 85.

14   "Narrow Flowers." *The Dial* 68.1 (January 1920): 73.

14   "After Youth." *The Dial* 68.1 (January 1920): 74.

16   "Air for G Strings." *The Dial* 69 (September 1920): 267-68.

17   "Destiny." *The Poetry Journal* 8 (1918): 86.

18   "Isolation Ward." *The Dial* 68.1 (January 1920): 75.

19   "The Red Cross." *The Dial* 68.1 (January 1920): 75.

21   "Spring Song." *The Dial* 49 (September 1920): 267.

27   "Ship Masts." *Poetry* 15.2 (November 1919): 73.

30   "The Storm." *Poetry* 15.2 (November 1919): 70-71.

33   Author's emendation from a personal copy of *Precipitations*, HRHRC Evelyn Scott Collection, back velvet>black velvet

34   "Designs." *The Dial* 68.1 (January 1920):71-72.

35   "Argo." *The Poetry Journal* 8 (1918): 85.

35   "Japanese Moon." *The Poetry Journal* 8 (1918): 86.

36   "The Naiad." *The Poetry Journal* 8 (1918): 85.

38   "Young Men." *Others* 5 (April-May 1919): 23.

38   "Young Girls." *Others* 5 (February 1919): 15.

38   "House Spirits." *Liberator* (February 1920): 45.

40   Author's emendation from a personal copy of *Precipitations*, HRHRC Evelyn Scott Collection, CHRISTIANS>PURITANS

40   Author's emendation from a personal copy of *Precipitations*, Robert Welker Private Collection, Columbine breeding>Columbine bleeding

40   "Devil's Cradle." *The Dial* 68.1 (January 1920): 74.

41 "Women." *Others* 5 (February 1919): 14-15.

41 "Penelope." *Others* 5 (April-May 1919): 22.

43 Author's emendation from a personal copy of *Precipitations*, HRHRC Evelyn Scott Collection, polish>polished

43 Author's emendation from a personal copy of *Precipitations*, Robert Welker Private Collection, polish floor>polished floor

44 Author's emendation from a personal copy of *Precipitations*, HRHRC Evelyn Scott Collection, Warm and snug is old lady's belly.>Warm and snug in old lady's belly,

44 "Nigger," *Precipitations*, Robert Welker Private Collection, "This was William Saphier as I saw him."

45 "A Very Old Rose Jar." *Playboy: A Portfolio of Art and Satire* 1 (1919):12.

47 Author's emendation from a personal copy of *Precipitations*, Robert Welker Private Collection, Your life for her—>Your life for hers—

48 *Precipitations*, HRHRC Evelyn Scott Collection, "W. C. Williams" next to II

48 *Precipitations* , Robert Welker Private Collection, "Portrait of W. C. Williams poet"; in the margin: "This was originally dedicated to W. C. Williams"

48 *Precipitations*, HRHRC Evelyn Scott Collection, "Alfred Kreymborg" next to III

48 *Precipitations*, Robert Welker Private Collection, "Portrait of William Saphir painter." In the margin of the Welker copy, "This was originally designated portrait of A. Kreymborg"

50 "Tropical Life" published as "Tropical Flowers." *Poetry* 15.2 (November 1919): 72.

50 "Twenty Four Hours." *Poetry* 15.2 (November 1919): 70.

50 "Rainy Season." *Poetry* 15.2 (November 1919): 71.

51 "Mail on the Ranch," *Precipitations*, Robert Welker Private Collection, "Like life in London, England 1944-1952". Published in *Poetry* 15.2 (November 1919): 72-3.

51 "The Vampire Bat." *Poetry* 15.2 (November 1919): 74-75.

52 "Conservatism," *Precipitations*, Robert Welker Private Collection, "Philistines, but just one so." Published in *Poetry* 15.2 (November 1919): 74.

52 "Little Pigs." *Poetry* 15.2 (November 1919): 75.

52 "The Silly Ewe." *Poetry* 15.2 (November 1919): 73-74.

53 "The Year." *Poetry* 15.2 (November 1919): 71-2.

57 "Guitarra" published as "Tropical Flowers." *Poetry* 15.2 (November 1919): 72.

60 *Precipitations*, HRHRC Evelyn Scott Collection, "written after a final quarrel with w.c.w. nyc Barrow st He had just left the house and I sat down and wrote this as it is"

61 "The Death of Columbine." *The Dial* 68.1 (January 1920): 73.

62   Author's emendation from a personal copy of *Precipitations*, HRHRC Evelyn Scott Collection, bubble light>bubble alight

65   "Immortality." *The Dial* 68.1 (January 1920): 76.

65   "Autumn Night," *The Dial* 68.1 (January 1920):72. Rpt. *Lyric America: 1630-1941*. Ed. by Alfred Kreymborg. NY: Tudor Publishing Co., 1941, 459.

84   A version of "Early Morning" was published as "Winter Morning," *Outlook* 55.1407 (Saturday, January 17, 1925): 40.

89   "The Mongoose," *New Republic* 59 (July 17, 1929): 227.

101 "Creatures in General." *The Second American Caravan*, ed. by Alfred Kreymborg et. al. New York: Macaulay Company, 1928, 625-26.

124 A version of "Joy" was published as "Touch," *Rhythmus* 1.2 (February 1923): 40.

129 "Burial" published as "Night." *The Poetry Journal* 8 (1918): 87.

131 Author's emendation from a personal copy of *The Winter Alone*, Robert Welker Private Collection, grisly> gristly

136 "Nirvana." *Outlook*. 55.1405 (Saturday, January 3, 1925): 8.

143 "Woman Cycle," *American Poetry Journal* (August 1933): 4-13.

152 "To a Snake in Eden." *Nation* 138 (2 February 1934): 225.

154 "Old American Stock." *Poetry Review* 42 (1951): 157-59.

159 "Pike's Peak" published as "To Zebulon Pike." *Contempo* 2.2 (May 25, 1932): 5.

160 "Apocrypha." *Saturday Review of Literature* 21 (February 17, 1940): 8.

162 "Innocent Life." *American Poetry Journal* (June 1934): 34.

167 "She Dies." *Saturday Review of Literature* 32 (January 29, 1949): 10.

176 "Opus Ten Billion." *North Georgia Review* 4 (Autumn 1939):42.

179 "Ennui" was previously published as "Ancient and Modern." *Windsor Quarterly* 1.1 (Spring 1933): 13. Also, *Pagany* 1-2 (April-June 1930):65.

181 Part 4 of "Ennui" published as "Progress," *American Poetry Journal* (June 1934): 34

192 "To Artists of Every Land." *Saturday Review of Literature* 31 (May 22, 1948): 20.

194 "Blue Moon" published as "Ivory Tower." *Poetry Review* 42.5 (September-October 1951): 283.

196 "Survival." *Saturday Review of Literature* 36 (June 6, 1953): 13.

207 "Fear." *Poetry* 15.2 (November 1919): 75.

207 "To a Blind Nazarene." *Double Blossoms: A Helen Keller Anthology*. New York: Copeland, 1931, 65.

208 "Chastity." *American Poetry Journal* (January 1935): 12.

INDEX OF TITLES AND FIRST LINES
(TITLES appear in ALL CAPITAL letters)